P2P Techniques
for Decentralized Applications

Synthesis Lectures on Data Management

Editor
M. Tamer Özsu, *University of Waterloo*

Synthesis Lectures on Data Management is edited by Tamer Özsu of the University of Waterloo. The series will publish 50- to 125 page publications on topics pertaining to data management. The scope will largely follow the purview of premier information and computer science conferences, such as ACM SIGMOD, VLDB-ICDE, PODS, ICDT, and ACM KDD. Potential topics include, but not are limited to: query languages, database system architectures, transaction management, data warehousing, XML and databases, data stream systems, wide scale data distribution, multimedia data management, data mining, and related subjects.

P2P Techniques for Decentralized Applications
Esther Pacitti, Reza Akbarinia, and Manal El-Dick
2012

Query Answer Authentication
HweeHwa Pang and Kian-Lee Tan
2012

Declarative Networking
Boon Thau Loo and Wenchao Zhou
2012

Full-Text (Substring) Indexes in External Memory
Marina Barsky, Ulrike Stege, and Alex Thomo
2011

Spatial Data Management
Nikos Mamoulis
2011

Database Repairing and Consistent Query Answering
Leopoldo Bertossi
2011

P2P Techniques for Decentralized Applications
Esther Pacitti, Reza Akbarinia, and Manal El-Dick

ISBN: 978-3-031-00760-6   paperback
ISBN: 978-3-031-01888-6   ebook

DOI 10.1007/978-3-031-01888-6

A Publication in the Springer series
SYNTHESIS LECTURES ON DATA MANAGEMENT

Lecture #25
Series Editor: M. Tamer Özsu, *University of Waterloo*
Series ISSN
Synthesis Lectures on Data Management
Print 2153-5418   Electronic 2153-5426

P2P Techniques
for Decentralized Applications

Esther Pacitti
INRIA and Lirmm, University of Montpellier 2, France

Reza Akbarinia
INRIA and Lirmm, Montpellier

Manal El-Dick
Lebanese University

SYNTHESIS LECTURES ON DATA MANAGEMENT #25

ABSTRACT

As an alternative to traditional client-server systems, Peer-to-Peer (P2P) systems provide major advantages in terms of scalability, autonomy and dynamic behavior of peers, and decentralization of control. Thus, they are well suited for large-scale data sharing in distributed environments. Most of the existing P2P approaches for data sharing rely on either structured networks (e.g., DHTs) for efficient indexing, or unstructured networks for ease of deployment, or some combination. However, these approaches have some limitations, such as lack of freedom for data placement in DHTs, and high latency and high network traffic in unstructured networks. To address these limitations, gossip protocols which are easy to deploy and scale well, can be exploited. In this book, we will give a overview of these different P2P techniques and architectures, discuss their trade-offs and illustrate their use for decentralizing several large-scale data sharing applications.

KEYWORDS

large scale data sharing, peer-to-peer systems, DHT, unstructuted overlays, gossip protocols, top-k queries, recommendation, content sharing, caching, CDN, on-line communities, social-networks, information retrieval

Contents

Preface

The Web 2.0 has brought a paradigm shift in how people use the Web. Before this Web evolution, users were merely passive consumers of content that is provided to them by a set of websites. In a nutshell, Web 2.0 offers an architecture of participation where individuals can participate, collaborate, share and create content. Web 2.0 applications deliver services that get better the more people use it, while providing their own content and remixing it with others content. Today, there are many emerging websites that have helped to pioneer the concept of participation in Web 2.0. Popular examples include the online encyclopedia Wikipedia that enables individuals to create and edit content (articles), social networking sites like Facebook, photo and video sharing sites like YouTube and Flickr, as well as wikis and blogs. Social networking is even allowing scientific groups to expand their knowledge base and share their theories which might otherwise become isolated and irrelevant.

With the Internet reaching a critical mass of users, Web 2.0 has encouraged the emergence of peer-to-peer (P2P) technology as a new communication model. The P2P model stands in direct contrast to the traditional client-server model, as it introduces symmetry in roles, where each peer is both a client and a server. Whereas a client-server network requires more investment to serve more clients, a P2P network pools the resources of each peer for the common good. In other terms, it exhibits the network effect as defined by economists: the value of a network to an individual user scales with the total number of participants. In theory, as the number of peers increases, the aggregate storage space and content availability grow linearly, the user-perceived response time remains constant, whereas the search throughput remains high or even grows. Therefore, it is commonly believed that P2P networks are naturally suited for handling large-scale applications, due to their inherent self-scalability. Since the late 1990s, P2P technology has gained popularity, mainly in the form of file sharing applications where peers exchange multimedia files. Chapter 1 covers the most relevant P2P concepts and overlays.

Under the Web 1.0 context, the content of web-servers is distributed to large audiences via Content Distribution Networks (CDN). The main mechanism is to replicate popular content at strategically placed and dedicated servers. As it intercepts and serves the clients queries, a CDN decreases the workload on the original web-servers, reduces bandwidth costs, and keeps the user-perceived latency low. Given that the Web is witnessing an explosive growth in the amount of web content and users, P2P networks seem to be the perfect match to build low cost infrastructures for content distribution. This is because they can offer several advantages like decentralization, self-organization, fault-tolerance and scalability. In a P2P system, users serve each other's queries by sharing their previously requested content, thus distributing the content without the need for powerful and dedicated servers. Chapter 2 presents an overview of P2P solutions for CDN decentralization over different P2P overlays.

More recently, P2P technologies have also been exploited for on-line communities, where participants are willing to post contents in order to share them. Interestingly, some on-line communities' participants prefer to keep and share their contents in their own workspace. For instance, in modern e-science, such as bio-informatics, physics and environmental science, scientists must deal with overwhelming amount of content (experimental data, documents, images, etc.) wishing to keep their contents in their own PC's instead of storing it in untrusted servers. Again, this seems a perfect match to P2P networks. P2P File-sharing systems have proven very efficient at locating content given specific queries. However, few solutions exist that are able to recommend the most relevant documents given a keyword-based query. This requires the use if recommendation methods. Chapter 3 presents some interesting P2P solutions for decentralized recommendation.

In very large-scale P2P systems, for each user's query there may be a huge number of answers most of which may be uninteresting for the user. Top-k queries have proved to be very useful to avoid overwhelming the user with large numbers of uninteresting answers. In addition, by filtering useless results they can significantly reduce the network traffic in P2P systems. By definition, a top-k query returns only the k data the most relevant to the users query. The relevance of data can be measured by a scoring function that the user specifies. In Chapter 4, we present some interesting approaches for top-k query processing in P2P networks.

A very interesting lecture on P2P Data Management can be found in Aberer [2010]. The authors focus on P2P management for data management, data integration and documents retrieval systems. Different from Aberer [2010], our goal is to show how different P2P technologies can be used generically for application decentralization focusing on Top-k, CDN and Recommendations systems.

Esther Pacitti, Reza Akbarinia, and Manal El-Dick
April 2012

Acknowledgments

We would like to acknowledge Fady Draidi for his very useful inputs for recommendation systems.

CHAPTER 1

P2P Overlays, Query Routing, and Gossiping

A P2P system is a distributed system in which the *peers* (nodes) are relatively autonomous and can join or leave the system anytime. By distributing data storage, processing and bandwidth across autonomous peers, P2P systems can usually scale up to a very large number of peers. They have been successfully used for sharing computation, e.g., Seti@home [Anderson et al., 2002] and Genome@home [Larson et al., 2003a], [Larson et al., 2003b], internet services, e.g., P2P multicast systems [Bhargava et al., 2004], or data, e.g., Gnutella[1].

There are several features that distinguish data management in P2P systems from traditional distributed database systems (DDBS), some of which are the following [Ng et al., 2003].

- Peers in P2P systems are very dynamic and can join and leave the system anytime. But, in a DDBS, nodes are added to and removed from the system in a controlled manner.

- Usually there is no predefined global schema for describing the data shared by the peers.

- In P2P systems, the answers to queries are typically incomplete. The reason is that some peers may be absent at query execution time. In addition, due to the very large scale of the network, forwarding a query to all peers can be very inefficient.

- In P2P systems, there is no centralized catalog that can be used to determine the peers that hold relevant data to a query. However, such a catalog is an essential component of DDBS.

In this chapter, we first give an overview of the existing P2P architectures, and compare their properties from the perspective of data management. Then, in Section 1.2, we present the algorithms that have been proposed for routing queries to relevant peers. In Section 1.3, we introduce the utilization of gossip protocols for data propagation in P2P systems. In Section 1.4, we introduce data replication in P2P systems. In Section 1.5, we discuss some advanced issues for data management in P2P systems, and in Section 1.6 we conclude.

1.1 P2P OVERLAYS

P2P systems are built on a P2P overlay, and the overlay is built on top of the physical network (typically the Internet). The topology of the P2P overlay strongly impacts the properties of the P2P

[1]http://www.gnutellaforums.com/. Accessed on October 2011

system, such as fault-tolerance, self-maintainability, performance and scalability. We consider three main P2P overlay architectures: unstructured, structured, and super-peer.

1.1.1   UNSTRUCTURED

In unstructured P2P overlays, the topology is managed in a random manner. Each peer knows some peers chosen usually randomly, and query routing is typically done by forwarding the query to the peers that are in limited hop distance from the query originator (see Section 1.2 for more details).

Usually, there is no restriction on the manner the queries are described, for example keyword search, SQL-like query, and other approaches can be used. Fault-tolerance is very high since all peers provide equal functionality and are able to replicate data. In addition, each peer is autonomous to decide which data to store.

The main problems of unstructured overlays are inefficient query routing and incompleteness of query results. Query routing mechanisms in unstructured overlays usually do not scale up to a large number of peers because of the huge amount of load they incur on the network. Also, the incompleteness of the results can be high since some peers containing relevant data may not be reached because they are too far away from the query originator.

Examples of P2P systems supported by unstructured overlay include Freenet [Clarke et al., 2002] and Gnutella (before v0.4).

1.1.2   STRUCTURED

Structured overlays try to be efficient in query routing by tightly controlling the overlay topology and data placement. Data (or pointers to them) are placed at precisely specified locations, and the routing of queries to the data is done efficiently.

Distributed hash table (DHT) is the main representative of structured overlays. While there are significant implementation differences between DHTs, they all map each given key into a peer p, called responsible for the key, using a hash function and can lookup p efficiently, usually in $O(log\ n)$ routing hops where n is the number of peers [Harren et al., 2002]. DHTs typically provide an operation *put(key, data)* that stores the *data* at the peer that is responsible for *key*. For requesting a data, there is an operation *get(key)* that routes the key to the peer that is responsible for it, and retrieves the requested data.

Because a peer is responsible for storing the values corresponding to its range of keys, autonomy is limited. Furthermore, DHT queries are typically limited to exact match keyword search. Much research has been done to extend the DHT capabilities to deal with more complex queries such as range queries [Gao and Steenkiste, 2004], join queries [Huebsch et al., 2003], and top-k queries [Akbarinia et al., 2007].

Examples of P2P systems supported by structured overlays include Chord [Stoica et al., 2001], CAN [Ratnasamy et al., 2001], Tapestry [Zhao et al., 2004], Pastry [Rowstron and Druschel, 2001b], Freenet [Clarke et al., 2002], PIER [Huebsch et al., 2003], OceanStore [Kubiatowicz et al., 2000], Past [Rowstron and Druschel, 2001c], and P-Grid [Aberer et al., 2003].

1.1.3   SUPER-PEER

Unstructured and structured architectures are considered as "pure" P2P overlays because all their peers provide the same functionality. In contrast, super-peer overlays are hybrid between client-server systems and pure P2P overlays. Like client-server systems, some peers, called *super-peers*, act as dedicated servers for some other peers and can perform complex functions such as indexing, query processing, access control, and meta-data management. Using only one super-peer reduces to client-server with all the problems associated with a single server. Like pure overlays, super-peers can be organized in a P2P fashion and communicate with one another in sophisticated ways, thereby allowing the partitioning or replication of global information across all super-peers. Super-peers can be dynamically elected (e.g., based on their bandwidth and processing power) and replaced in the presence of failures.

In a super-peer overlay, a requesting peer simply sends the request, which can be expressed in a high-level language, to its responsible super-peer. The super-peer can then find the relevant peers either directly through its index or indirectly using its neighbor super-peers.

The main advantages of super-peer overlays are efficiency and quality of service. The time needed to find data by directly accessing indices in a super-peer is very small compared with query routing in unstructured overlays. In addition, super-peer overlays exploit and take advantage of different peers' capabilities in terms of CPU power, bandwidth, or storage capacity as super-peers take on a large portion of the entire network load. In contrast, in pure overlays, all nodes are equally loaded regardless of their capabilities. Access control can also be better enforced since directory and security information can be maintained at the super-peers. However, autonomy is restricted since peers cannot log in freely to any super-peer. Fault-tolerance is typically low since super-peers are single points of failure for their sub-peers (dynamic replacement of super-peers can alleviate this problem).

Examples of super-peer systems include Edutella [Nejdl et al., 2003], Publius [Waldman et al., 2000], and JXTA[2]. A more recent version of Gnutella also relies on super-peers [Androutsellis-Theotokis and Spinellis, 2004a].

1.1.4   COMPARING P2P OVERLAYS

From the perspective of data management, the main requirements of a P2P system are [Daswani et al., 2003]: autonomy, query expressiveness, efficiency, quality of service, fault-tolerance, and security. Below, we describe these requirements, and then compare P2P overlays based on these requirements.

- **Autonomy.** An autonomous peer should be able to join or leave the system at any time, and to be connected to any peer it wants.

- **Query expressiveness.** The query language should allow the user to describe the desired data at the appropriate level of detail. The simplest form of query is keyword search that is only

---

[2]http://jxta.kenai.com/. Accessed on November 2011

appropriate for finding files. But for more structured data, an SQL-like query language is necessary.

- **Efficient query processing.** The efficient use of the P2P overlay resources (bandwidth, computing power, storage) should result in low response time of queries.

- **Quality of service.** Refers to the user-perceived efficiency of the P2P system, e.g., completeness of query results, query response time, etc.

- **Fault-tolerance.** Services should be guaranteed under some conditions, despite the occurrence of peer failures.

Table 1.1 summarizes how the requirements for data management are possibly attained by the three main classes of P2P overlays. This is a rough comparison to understand the respective merits of each class. For instance, high means it can be high. Obviously, there is room for improvement in each class of P2P overlays. For instance, fault-tolerance can be made higher in super-peers by relying on replication and fail-over techniques.

Table 1.1: Comparison of P2P overlays			
Requirements	**Unstructured**	**Structured**	**Super-peer**
Autonomy	high	low	moderate
Query expressiveness	high	low	high
Efficient query processing	low	high	high
QoS	low	high	high
Fault tolerance	high	high	low

1.2   QUERY ROUTING

One of the main questions for query processing in P2P systems is how to route the query to relevant peers, i.e., those that hold some data related to the query [Li and Wu, 2006]. Once the query is routed to relevant peers, it is executed at those peers and the answers are returned to the query originator.

In this section, we describe the approaches for query routing in unstructured, DHT, and super-peer overlays.

1.2.1   QUERY ROUTING IN UNSTRUCTURED OVERLAYS

The approaches used in unstructured overlays for query routing can be classified as [Tsoumakos and Roussopoulos, 2003b]: Breath-First Search (BFS), iterative deepening, random walks, adaptive probabilistic search, local indices, bloom filter based indices, and distributed resource location protocol.

BFS

This approach floods the query to all accessible peers within a TTL (Time To Live) hop distance as follows. Whenever a query with a TTL is issued at a peer, called query originator, it is forwarded to all its neighbors. Each peer, which receives the query, decreases the TTL by one and if it is greater than one sends the query and TTL to its neighbors. By continuing this procedure, all accessible peers whose hop distance from the query originator is less than or equal to TTL receive the query. Each peer that receives the query executes it locally and returns the answers directly to the query originator (see Figure 1.1).

Modified BFS [Kalogeraki et al., 2002] is a variation of the BFS approach in which the peers randomly choose only a subset of their neighbors and forward the query only to these neighbors. Although this approach reduces the number of messages needed for query routing, it may loose many of the good answers that could be found by BFS.

Intelligent BFS [Kalogeraki et al., 2002] is another variation. For each recently answered query, peers maintain statistics about the query and the number of answers that are found via each of their neighbors. When a peer receives a query, it identifies all queries similar to the received query, e.g., using a query similarity metric, and sends the query to a set of its neighbors that have returned most of the answers for similar queries. If an answer is found for the query at a peer, a message is sent to the peers over the reverse path in order to update their statistics. Like standard BFS, each peer that receives the query decreases the TTL by one, and if it is equal to zero, the query is discarded. Compared to modified BFS, intelligent BFS can find better answers. However, it produces more routing messages, because of messages sent to update statistics. In addition, it can not be easily adapted to the peer departures and data deletions.

Iterative Deepening

Iterative deepening [Yang and Garcia-Molina, 2002] is used when the user is satisfied by only one answer or a small number answer. In this algorithm, the query originator performs consecutive BFS searches such that the first BFS has a low TTL, e.g., 1, and each new BFS uses a TTL greater than the previous one. The algorithm ends when the required number of answers is found or a BFS with the predefined maximum TTL is done. For the cases where a sufficient number of answers are available at the peers that are close to the query originator, this algorithm achieves good performance gains compared to the standard BFS. In other cases, its overhead and response time may be much higher than the standard BFS.

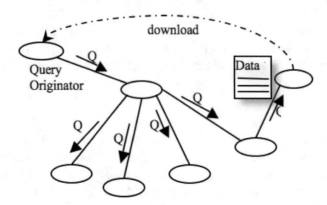

Figure 1.1: Example of BFS. The received query is forwarded to all neighbors.

Random Walks

In Random Walks [Lv et al., 2002], for each query, the query originator forwards k query messages to k of its randomly chosen neighbors. Each of these messages follows its own path, having intermediate peers forward it to a randomly chosen neighbor at each step (see Figure 1.2). These messages are known as *walkers*. When the TTL of a walker reaches zero, it is discarded.

Let k be the number of walkers. The main advantage of the Random Walks algorithm is that it produces $k \times TTL$ routing messages in the worst case, a number that does not depend on the underlying network. Performance evaluation results in [Lv et al., 2002] show that routing messages can be reduced significantly compared to the standard BFS. The main disadvantage of this algorithm is its highly variable performance, because the number of successfully answered queries vary greatly depending on overlay topology and the random choices. Another drawback of this method is that it cannot learn anything from its previous successes or failures.

Adaptive Probabilistic Search

In Adaptive Probabilistic Search (APS) [Tsoumakos and Roussopoulos, 2003a], for each recently requested data, the peers maintain the data identifier and probability of returning the data by each of their neighbors. Given a query, the query originator establishes k independent walkers and sends them to its neighbors. Each intermediate peer, which receives a walker, sends it to the neighbor that has the highest probability to return the requested data. Initially equal for all neighbors, the probability values are updated using either an optimistic or a pessimistic approach. In the optimistic approach, when a peer sends a walker to a neighbor, it increases in advance the corresponding probability value. However, if the walker terminates without the requested data, a message is sent over the walker path to decrease the corresponding probability values. The pessimistic approach makes the assumption that the data cannot be found, so it decreases the corresponding probability

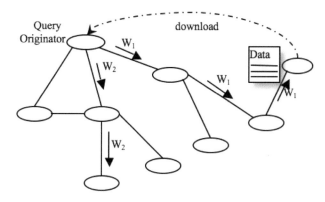

Figure 1.2: Example of Random Walks: each received walk is forwarded to only one neighbor.

value after sending the walker to a neighbor. If the walker finds the data, all peers over the walker path update their probability values by increasing them.

To remember a walker's path, each peer appends its ID in the query message during query forwarding. If a walker w_2 passes by a peer where another walker w_1 stopped before, the walker w_2 terminates unsuccessfully. APS has very good performance as it is bandwidth-efficient: the number of routing messages produced by it is very close to that of Random Walks. In spite of this, the probability of finding the requested data by APS is much higher than that of Random Walks. However, if the topology of the P2P system changes quickly, the ability of APS to answer queries reduces significantly.

Local Indices

In this approach [Crespo and Garcia-Molina, 2002, Yang and Garcia-Molina, 2002], each peer p indexes the data shared by all peers that are within a radius r, i.e., the peers whose hop-distance from p is less than or equal to r. The query routing is done in a BFS-like way, except that the query is processed only at the peers that are at certain hop distances from the query originator. To minimize the query processing overhead, the hop distance between two consecutive peers that process the query must be $2 \times r + 1$. In other words, the query must be processed at peers whose distance from the query originator is $m \times (2 \times r + 1)$ for $m = 1, 2, \ldots$. This allows querying all data without any overlap. The query processing cost of this approach is less than that of standard BFS because only some peers process the query. However, the number of routing messages is comparable to that of standard BFS. In addition, whenever a peer joins/leaves the system or updates its shared data, a flooding with $TTL = r$ is needed in order to update the peers indices, so the overhead becomes very significant for highly dynamic environments.

Bloom Filter based Indices

In [Rhea and Kubiatowicz, 2002], the indexing of data is done using Bloom filters [Bloom, 1970]. Each peer holds d Bloom filters for each neighbor, such that the ith filter summarizes the data that can be found i hops away through that specific neighbor. When a peer receives a query, it checks its local data and returns the answers to the query originator. Then, it forwards the query to the neighbor who has the minimum numbered filter involving the data.

The advantage of representing the indexed data by Bloom filters is that they are space efficient, i.e., with a small space, one can index a large number of data. However, it is possible that a Bloom filter gives a false positive answer, i.e., the Bloom filter wrongly returns a positive answer in response to a question asking the membership of a data item.

Distributed Resource Location Protocol

In Distributed Resource Location Protocol (DRLP) [Menascé and Kanchanapalli, 2002], the peers index the location of all data that are answer for recently issued queries. The indexing is done gradually as follows. Peers with no information about the location of a requested data forward the query to a set of randomly chosen neighbors. If the data is found at some peer, a message is sent over the reverse path to the query originator, in order to inform the peers on the path about the data location. In subsequent requests, peers with indexed location information forward the query directly to the relevant peers. This algorithm initially sends many messages for query routing. In subsequent requests, it might take only one message to discover the data. Thus, if a query is issued frequently, this approach is very efficient.

1.2.2   QUERY ROUTING IN DHTS

The way by which a DHT routes the keys to their responsible peers depends on the DHT's *routing geometry*, i.e., the topology that is used by the DHT for arranging peers and routing queries over them. The routing geometries in DHTs include the following [Gummadi et al., 2003]: tree, hypercube, ring, butterfly, and hybrid. Let us describe these geometries and discuss their query routing approaches.

Tree

Tree is one of the first geometries used for organizing the peers of a DHT and routing queries among them. In this geometry, the identifiers of peers constitute the leaves of a binary tree with n nodes. The responsible for a given key is the peer whose identifier has the highest number of common prefix bits with the key. Let $h(p, q)$ be the number of common prefix bits between the identifiers of two peers p and q. For each i (with $0 \leq i \leq log\ n$), each peer p knows the address of a peer q such that $h(p, q) = i$. The routing of a key proceeds by doing a longest prefix match at each intermediate peer until reaching to the peer that has the most common prefix bit with the key. Let us illustrate the tree geometry by using an example.

Example 1.1   Consider the tree geometry in Figure 1.3, and assume the identifiers of peers $p_0, p_1, \ldots, p_7$ are $000, 001, \ldots, 111$, respectively. The routing table of each peer is shown below it. In the routing table of each peer p there should be at least one peer that has i common prefix bits with p, where $i = 0, \ldots, \log n$. For example, in the routing table of p_0 there is one peer with 0 common prefix bit (it can be one of peers p_4, p_5, p_6 or p_7), one peer with 1 common prefix bit (it can be p_2 or p_3), and one peer with two common prefix bits (i.e., p_1). Let us now consider the routing of a key $k = 1001$ from p_0. The peer that is responsible for maintaining k is p_4, because its identifier has the highest number of common prefix bits with k. To route k, p_0 looks at its routing table and sends k and its associated data to the peer that has the largest common prefixes with k. In its routing table, the only peer whose identifier has a common prefix with k is p_7. Thus, k is sent to p_7 who sends it to p_5 (there is two common prefix bits between k and id of p_5). Then p_5 sends the key and its associated data to p_4.

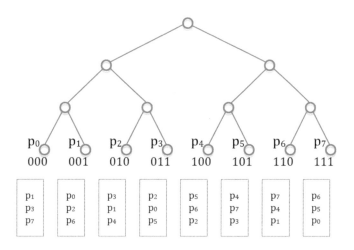

Figure 1.3: Example of tree routing geometry: the identifier and routing table of each peer is shown below it.

The basic routing algorithms in Tapestry [Zhao et al., 2004] is rather similar to this algorithm. In Tapestry, each identifier is associated with a node that is the root of a spanning tree used to route messages for the given identifier.

Hypercube

The hypercube geometry is based on partitioning a d-dimensional space into a set of separate zones and attributing each zone to one peer. Peers have unique identifiers with $\log n$ bits, where n is the total number of peers of the hypercube. The *distance* between two peers is the number of bits on which their identifiers differ. The neighbors of each peer p are the peers whose distance from it is one. In other words, there is only one different bit between the identifier of p and each of its neighbors. For example, in Figure 1.4, the neighbors of the peer with $id = 000$ are those whose ids are 001, 010, and 100.

Query routing in hypercube geometry proceeds by greedily forwarding the given key via intermediate peers to the peer that has minimum bit difference with the key. Thus, it is somehow similar to routing on the tree geometry. The difference is that the hypercube allows bit differences to be reduced in any order while with the tree, bit differences have to be reduced in strictly left-to-right order.

Example 1.2   Consider the hypercube shown in Figure 1.4, and assume we want to route a key $k = 110$ from the peer whose id is 000. The responsible for k is the peer whose id is 110. To route the key, peer 000 sends it to one of its neighbors that have minimum distance with the key (it can be one of the peers 100 or 010). Assume its selects the peer 010, and sends k to it. Then, the peer 010 sends the key to the peer 110 that is one of its neighbors.

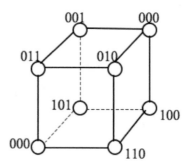

Figure 1.4: Example of hypercube routing geometry.

The routing geometry used in CAN [Ratnasamy et al., 2001] resembles a hypercube geometry. CAN uses a d-dimensional coordinate space that is partitioned into n zones and each zone is occupied by one peer. When $d = log\ n$, the neighbor sets in CAN are similar to those of a $log\ n$ dimensional hypercube.

Ring

In Ring geometry, the peers are ordered on the circle clockwise with respect to their identifiers. Chord [Stoica et al., 2001] is a DHT protocol that relies on this geometry for query routing. In Chord, each peer has an m-bit identifier, and the responsible for a key k is the first peer whose identifier is equal or follows k. Each peer p knows the address of the peers whose distance from p clockwise in the circle is 2^i, for $0 \le i < log\ n$. Using this topology, any peer can route its messages to any other peer in at most $log\ n$ hops because each hop cuts the distance to the destination at least by half.

Example 1.3   Figure 1.5 shows an example of Chord with 8 peers. Each peer knows the peers whose clockwise distance from it is 2^i, for i=0, 1,2. For example, peer 1 knows peers 2, 3, and 5. Let us now consider the routing of a message from peers 1–7. To do so, peer 1 sends the message to the neighbor that is the nearest to the destination, that is peer 5. Then, peer 5 sends the message to peer 7 directly. Notice that peer 5 knows the address of peer 7, because their clockwise distance is 2^1.

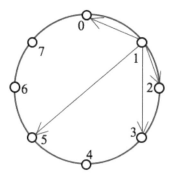

Figure 1.5: Example of ring routing geometry: the fleshes show the path for sending a message from peers 1–7.

Butterfly

The Butterfly geometry is an extension of the traditional butterfly network that supports the scalability requirements of DHTs. Viceroy [Malkhi et al., 2002] is a DHT that uses this geometry for efficient data location. The peers of a butterfly with size n are portioned into $log\ n$ levels and $n/log\ n$ rows (see Figure 1.6). The peers of each row are subsequently connected to each other using successor/predecessor links. The number of peers in each row is $log\ n$, thus a sequential lookup in each row is done in $O(log\ n)$. In addition to successor/predecessor links, each peer has some links to the peers of other rows. The inter-row links are arranged in such a way that the distance between a peer in Level 1 of any row to any other row is $log\ n$. Routing a query in the Butterfly is done in three steps as follows.

- **Step 1.** the query is sequentially forwarded to the peer that is at Level 1 of the row that contains query originator. This is done in $O(log\ n)$ routing hops.

- **Step 2.** from Level 1, the query is routed in $O(log\ n)$ routing hops to the row to which the destination peer belongs.

- **Step 3.** at the destination row, the query is forwarded sequentially to the destination peer.

Each of these steps is done in $O(log\ n)$ routing hops, thus the total time of query routing is $O(log\ n)$. The advantages of the Butterfly geometry is that the size of the routing table per peer, i.e., the number of neighbors of each peer, is a small constant number, whereas in most of other geometries this size is $O(log\ n)$. However, in Butterfly there is only one choice for selecting the neighbors or the route.

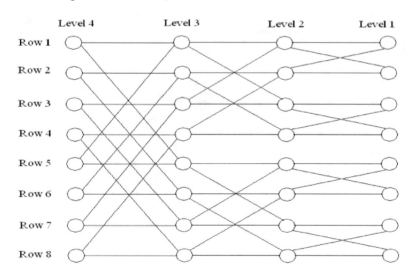

Figure 1.6: Butterfly routing geometry.

Hybrid

Hybrid geometries use a combination of the basic geometries. Pastry [Rowstron and Druschel, 2001b] combines the tree and ring geometries in order to achieve more efficiency and flexibility. Peer identifiers are maintained as both the leaves of a binary tree and as points on a one-dimensional circle. In Pastry, the distance between a given pair of nodes is computed in two different ways: the tree distance and the ring distance. Peers have great flexibility of neighbor selection. For selecting their neighbors, peers take into account the proximity properties, i.e., they select the neighbors that are close to them in the underlying physical network. The route selection is also very flexible, because to route a message peers have the possibility to choose one of the hops that do make progress on the tree or on the ring.

1.2.3   QUERY ROUTING IN SUPER-PEERS

Super-peer overlays typically rely on some powerful and highly available peers, called *super-peers*, to index the data shared by peers. Edutella is one of the most known super-peer overlays. In Edutella, super-peers are arranged in the hypercube topology [Schlosser et al., 2002] (see Figure 1.7), so messages can be communicated between any two super-peers in $O(log\ m)$ routing hops, where m is the number of super-peers. The process of joining a super-peer to the system consists of two parts: taking the appropriate position in the hypercube topology and announcing itself to its neighbors. Each ordinary peer joins the system by connecting to a super-peer.

To support efficient query routing, at each super-peer two kinds of routing indices are maintained: *super-peer/peer (SP/P)* indices and *super-peer/super-peer (SP/SP)* indices. Queries are routed over super-peers by using the SP/SP indices, and to ordinary peers based on the SP/P indices.

In the SP/P indices, each super-peer stores information about the characteristics of the data shared by the peers that are connected to it. These indices are used to route a query from the super-peer to its connected peers. At join time, peers provide their metadata information to their super-peer by publishing an advertisement. To index the provided metadata, Edutella uses the schema-based approaches that have successfully been used in the context of mediator-based information systems (e.g., [Wiederhold, 1992]). To ensure that the indices are always up-to-date, peers notify super-peers when their data change. When a peer leaves the system, all references to this peer are removed from the indices. If a super-peer fails, its formerly connected peers must connect to another super-peer chosen at random, and provide their metadata to it.

SP/SP indices are essentially summaries (possibly also approximations) of SP/P indices. Update of SP/SP indices is triggered after any modification to SP/P indices as follows. When a super-peer changes its SP/P index, e.g., due to a peer's join/leave, it broadcasts an announcement of update to the super-peer overlay by using the hypercube topology. The other super-peers update their SP/SP indices accordingly. Although such a broadcast is not optimal, it is not too costly either because the number of super-peers is much less than the number of all peers. Furthermore, if peers join/leave frequently, the super-peer can send a summary announcement periodically instead of sending a separate announcement for each join/leave.

The query routing in Edutella is done as follows. When a peer receives a query issued by the user, it sends the query to its super-peer. At the super-peer, the metadata used in the query are matched against the SP/P indices in order to determine local peers that are able to answer the query. If the query cannot be satisfied by local peers, it is forwarded to other super-peers using SP/SP indices.

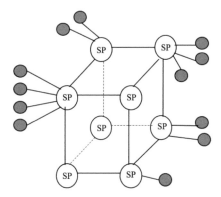

Figure 1.7: Edutella architecture.

1.3 GOSSIP PROTOCOLS

Gossip protocols are widely used for information dissemination in P2P systems. They can serve as efficient tools to achieve new P2P trends in a scalable and robust manner. Gossip protocols have recently received considerable attention from researchers in the field of P2P systems [Kermarrec and van Steen, 2007]. In addition to their inherent scalability, they are simple to implement, robust and resilient to failures. They are designed to deal with continuous changes in the system, while they exhibit reliability despite peer failures and message loss. This makes them ideally suited for large-scale and dynamic environments like P2P systems. In this section, we provide generic definition and description of gossip protocols, then we investigate how P2P systems can leverage these protocols.

Gossip algorithms mimic rumor mongering in real life. Just as people pass on a rumor by gossiping to their contacts, each peer in a distributed system relays new information it has received to selected peers which in their turn, forward the information to other peers, and so on. They are also known as *epidemic protocols* in reference to virus spreading [Demers et al., 1987].

The generic gossip behavior of each peer can be modeled by means of two separate threads: an *active thread* which takes the initiative of communication and a *passive thread* which reacts to incoming initiatives [Kermarrec and van Steen, 2007]. Peers communicate to exchange information that depends strictly on the application. The information exchange can be performed via two strategies : *push* and *pull*. A push occurs in the active thread, i.e., the peer that initiates gossiping shares its information upon contacting the remote peer. A pull occurs in the passive thread, i.e., the peer shares its information upon being contacted by the initiating peer. A gossip protocol can either adopt one of these strategies or the combination of both (i.e., *push-pull* which implies a mutual exchange of information during each gossip communication).

Figure 1.8 illustrates in more detail a generic gossip exchange. Each peer A knows a group of other peers or *contacts* and stores pointers to them in its *view*. Also, A locally maintains information denoted as its *state* which is defined by the application (e.g., information about the data shared by A's contacts or simply information about the contacts). Periodically, A selects a contact B from its view to initiate a gossip communication. In a pull-push scheme, A selects some of its information and sends them to B which, in its turn, does the same. Upon receiving the remote information, each one of A and B merges it with its local information and update their state. At that point, the way a peer deals with the received information and accordingly update its local state is highly application dependent.

Gossip protocols may achieve four main purposes [Kermarrec and van Steen, 2007]: *dissemination*, *resource monitoring*, *topology construction*, and *peer sampling*. Figure 1.9 illustrates these gossip-based services and how they interfere in a P2P system that is represented by an overlay layer and a search layer.

Introduced by Demers et al. [Demers et al., 1987], dissemination has traditionally been the purpose of gossiping. In short, the aim [Eugster et al., 2004] is to spread some new information throughout the network by letting peers forward messages to each other. The information gets

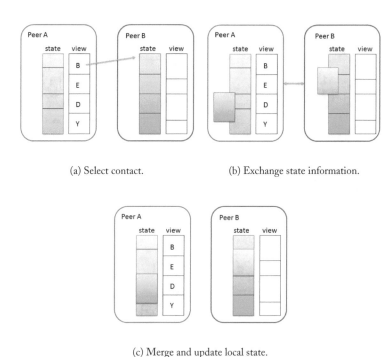

(a) Select contact.   (b) Exchange state information.

(c) Merge and update local state.

Figure 1.8: Peer A gossiping to peer B.

propagated exponentially through the network. In general, it takes $O(log\ N)$ rounds to reach all peers, where N is the number of peers. Figure 1.9 shows that gossip-based dissemination can be used to feed the search layer with indexing information useful to route queries. Basically, a peer can maintain and gossip information about the data stored by other peers and decide accordingly to which peers it should send a query.

Furthermore, gossip protocols have turned out to be a vehicle of resource monitoring in highly dynamic environments. It can be used to detect peer failures [Renesse et al., 1998], where each peer is in charge of monitoring its contacts, thus ensuring a fair balance of the monitoring cost. Further, gossip-based monitoring can guarantee that no node is left unattended, resulting in a robust self-monitoring system. In Figure 1.9, the monitoring service is used to maintain the overlay under churn by monitoring a peer's neighbors. In addition, it interferes in the search layer to monitor indexing information in face of data updates and peer failures.

Recently, various researches have explored gossip protocols as a means for overlay construction and maintenance according to certain desirable topologies (e.g., interest-based, locality-based, random graphs), without requiring any global information or centralized administration. In such systems, peers self-organize under the target topology, via a selection function that determines which

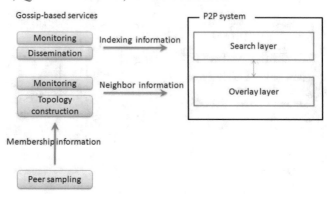

Figure 1.9: How a P2P system can leverage gossiping.

neighbors are optimal for each peer (e.g., semantic or physical proximity). Along these lines, several protocols have been proposed such as Vicinity [Voulgaris and van Steen, 2005] which creates a semantic overlay and T-Man [Jelasity and Babaoglu, 2005] that provides a general framework for creating topologies according to some ranking function. Figure 1.9 represents the topology construction service providing peers with specific neighbors and thereby connecting the P2P overlay.

Analyses [Jelasity et al., 2004] of gossip protocols reveal a high reliability and efficiency, under the assumption that the peers to send gossip messages to are selected uniformly at random from the set of all participant peers. This requires that a peer knows every other peer, i.e., that the peer has *global knowledge of the membership*, which is not feasible in a dynamic and large-scale P2P environment. Peer sampling offers a scalable and efficient alternative that continuously supplies a node with new and random samples of peers. This is achieved by gossiping membership information itself which is represented by the set of contacts in a peer's view. Basically, peers exchange their view information, thus discovering new contacts and accordingly updating their views. In order to preferentially select peers as neighbors, gossip-based overlay construction may be layered on top of a peer sampling service that returns uniformly and randomly selected peers. Well-known protocols of peer sampling are Lpbcast, Newscast, and Cyclon [Voulgaris et al., 2005]. In Figure 1.9, we can see the peer sampling service supporting other gossip-based services and supplying them with samples of peers from the network.

To conclude this section on gossip protocols, we briefly discuss their strengths and weaknesses.

- **Strengths.** Gossip algorithms have the advantage of being extremely simple to implement and configure [Birman, 2007]. Furthermore, they perfectly meet the decentralization requirement of P2P systems since many of them are designed in a way to let peers take local-only decisions. If properly designed, they can balance and limit the loads over participant peers.

Gossip protocols also provides high robustness which stems from the repeated probabilistic exchange of information between two peers [Kermarrec and van Steen, 2007]. Probabilistic choice refers to the choice of peer pairs that communicate while repetition refers to the endless process of choosing two peers to exchange information. Therefore, gossip protocols are resilient to failures and frequent changes and they cope well with the dynamic changes in P2P systems.

- **Weaknesses.** The usage of gossip might introduce serious limitations [Birman, 2007], e.g., the protocol running times can be slow and potentially costly in terms of background messages. One should carefully tune gossip parameters (e.g., periodicity) in a way that matches the goals of the target application.

1.4   REPLICATION

In the context of distributed systems, replication is commonly used to improve data availability and enhance performance. More particularly, P2P systems can significantly benefit from replication given the high levels of dynamicity and failures. For instance, if one peer is unavailable, its data can still be retrieved from the other peers that hold replicas. Data replication in P2P systems can be categorized as follows [Androutsellis-Theotokis and Spinellis, 2004b].

- **Passive Replication.** It refers to the replication of data that occurs naturally in P2P systems as peers request and download data. This technique perfectly complies with the autonomy of peers.

- **Active (or Proactive) Replication.** This technique consists in monitoring traffic and requests, and accordingly creating replicas of data objects to accommodate future demand.

To improve object availability and at the same time avoid hotspots, most DHT-based systems replicate popular objects and map the replicas to multiple peers. Generally, this can be done via two techniques. The first one [Ratnasamy et al., 2001] uses several hash functions to map the object to several keys and thereby store copies at several peers. The second technique consists in replicating the object in a number of peers whose IDs match most closely the key (or in other terms, in the logical neighborhood of the peer whose ID is the closest to the key). The latter technique is commonly used in several systems (e.g. [Dabek et al., 2001, Rowstron and Druschel, 2001d]).

Cohen and Shenker [2002] evaluate three different strategies for replication in an unstructured overlays. The *uniform strategy* creates a fixed number of copies when the object first enters the system. The *proportional strategy* creates a fixed number of copies every time the object is queried. In the *square-root replication strategy*, the number of copies for an object is proportional to the square root of its query probability. To implement these strategies, the object can be replicated either randomly or at peers along the path from the requester peer (i.e., the peer that submits the query) to the provider peer (i.e., the peer that stores the queried data). However, it is not clear how the strategies can be implemented in a decentralized way (e.g., how to monitor query rate under P2P dynamicity).

Further, such proactive replication is not feasible in systems that wish to respect peer autonomy because some peers may not want to store unrequested objects.

1.5   ADVANCED FEATURES ON P2P OVERLAYS

We have, so far, discussed P2P overlays from a classical perspective. However, research has evolved towards more sophisticated issues that could bring great benefits to data management in P2P applications.

1.5.1   LOCALITY-AWARE OVERLAYS

As introduced previously, peers are connected via a logical network superposed over the existing Internet infrastructure. This might cause a mismatch between the P2P overlay and the underlying Internet, which is clearly illustrated in Figure 1.10. As an example, peer A has peer B as its overlay neighbor while peer C is its physical neighbor. This can lead to inefficient routing in the overlay because any application-level path from peer A towards the nearby peer C traverses distant peers.

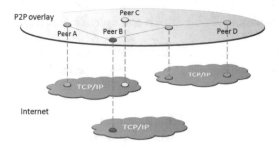

Figure 1.10: P2P overlay on top of the Internet infrastructure.

More precisely, the scalability of a P2P system is ultimately determined by its efficient use of underlying resources. The topology mismatch problem imposes substantial load on the underlying network infrastructure, which can eventually limit the scalability [Ripeanu et al., 2002a]. Furthermore, it can severely deteriorate the performance of search and routing techniques, typically by incurring long latencies and excessive traffic. Indeed, many studies [Saroiu et al., 2002] have revealed that the P2P traffic contributes the largest portion of the Internet traffic and acts as a leading consumer of Internet bandwidth. Thus, a fundamental challenge is to incorporate IP-level topological information in the construction of the overlay in order to improve routing and search performance. This optimization is referred to by *locality-awareness* since it deals with peers close in locality. In Chapter 2, we focus on locality-awareness as an important requirement of P2P applications such as P2P content distribution.

Below, we present the main approaches that incorporate locality-awareness in the overlay construction.

Clustering

[Krishnamurthy et al., 2001] consists of grouping physically close peers into clusters. The approach relies on a centralized engine to identify clusters of close peers under common administrative control. To achieve this, the central server uses IP-level routing information which is not directly available to end-user applications. Thus, the main drawbacks of this approach are the centralized topology control and the topological information itself, which prevents it from being scalable and fault-tolerant.

LTM Technique

[Liu et al., 2005] targets unstructured overlays and dynamically adapts connections between peers in a completely decentralized way. Each peer issues a detector in a small region so that the peers receiving the detector can record the relative delay. Accordingly, a receiving peer can detect and cut most of the inefficient logical links and add closer peers as neighbors. However, this scheme operates on long-time scales where the overlay is slowly improved over time. Given that participants join and leave on short time-scales, a solution that operates on long-time scales would be continually reacting to fluctuating peer membership without stabilizing.

Locality-Aware Structured Overlays

While the original versions of structured overlays did not take locality-awareness into account, almost all of the current versions make some attempt to deal with this primary issue. [Ratnasamy et al., 2002b] identifies three main approaches.

- *Geographic layout.* The peer IDs are assigned in a manner that ensures that peers that are close in the physical network are close in the peer identifier space.

- *Proximity routing.* The routing tables are built without locality-awareness but the routing algorithm aims at selecting, at each hop, the nearest peer among the ones in the routing table.

- *Proximity neighbor selection.* The construction of routing tables takes locality-awareness into account. When several candidate peers are available for a routing table entry, a peer prefers the one that is close in locality.

Pastry [Rowstron and Druschel, 2001a] and Tapestry [Zhao et al., 2004] adopt proximity neighbor selection. In order to preferentially select peers and fill routing tables, these systems assume the existence of a function (e.g., *Round-Trip-Time RTT*) that allows each peer to determine the physical distance between itself and any another peer. Although this solution leads to much shorter query routes, it requires expensive maintenance mechanisms as peers arrive and leave.

A design improvement of CAN aims at achieving geographic layout [Ratnasamy et al., 2002a]. It relies on a set of well-known landmarks spread across the network. A peer measures its RTT to the set of landmarks and orders them by increasing latency (i.e., network distance). The logical address space of CAN is then divided into bins such that each possible landmark ordering is represented by a bin. Physically close nodes are likely to have the same ordering and hence will belong to the same bin. This is illustrated in Figure 1.11. We have 3 landmarks (i.e., L1, L2, and L3) and, accordingly, the CAN coordinate space is divided into 6 bins (3! = 6). Since peers N1, N2, and N3 are physically close (see Figure 1.11 (a)), such peers produce the same landmark ordering, i.e., $L3 < L1 < L2$. As a result, N1, N2, and N3 are placed in the same bin of the overlay (see Figure 1.11 (b)). Notice that such approach is not perfect. For instance, peer N10 is closer to N3 than N5 in the physical network whereas the opposite situation is observed in the overlay. Despite its limited accuracy, binning has the advantage of being simple to implement and scalable since peers independently discover their bins without communicating with other participants. Furthermore, it does not incur high load on the landmark machines: they need only echo *ping* messages and do not actively initiate measurements nor manage measurement information. To achieve more scalability, multiple close-by nodes can act as a single logical landmark.

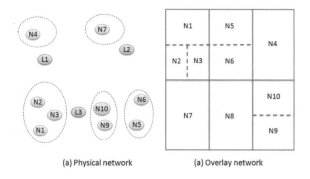

(a) Physical network   (a) Overlay network

Figure 1.11: Locality-aware construction of CAN.

1.5.2   INTEREST-BASED OVERLAYS

In attempt to improve the efficiency of search mechanisms, some works have addressed the arbitrary neighborhood of peers from a semantic perspective. Several measurement studies [Fessant et al., 2004, Handurukande et al., 2004, Sripanidkulchai et al., 2003b] of P2P workloads have demonstrated the inherent presence of *semantic proximity* between peers, i.e., similar interests between peers. They reached the following conclusion: "If a peer has an object that I am interested in, it is very likely that he will have other objects that I am (or will be) interested in." Moreover, they have shown that exploiting the implicit interest-based relationships between peers may lead to improvements in the search process. In Chapters 2 and 3, we discuss how P2P applications that are concerned with content sharing (i.e., P2P content distribution, recommendation) can greatly benefit from interest-based schemes.

1.5.3   P2P OVERLAY COMBINATION

Recently, some have started to justify that unstructured and structured overlays are complementary, not competing. It is actually easy to demonstrate that depending on the application, one or the other type of overlay is clearly more appropriate. In order to make use of the desirable features provided by each topology, there are efforts underway for combining both in the same P2P system. The combination might involve structured and unstructured overlays as well as interest- and locality-based overlays. Indeed, we show in Chapter 2 that a P2P content distribution system might need an interest-based overlay to cope with peer autonomy as well as a locality-aware overlay to achieve quality of service.

However, the construction and maintenance of the combined overlays might imply additional overhead which should not compromise the desirable gains. Below, we present and discuss some exemplary approaches.

Structured & Unstructured

Structella [Castro et al., 2004] improves the unstructured Gnutella system by adding some structural components. The motivation is that unstructured routing mechanisms can support complex queries but generate significant message overhead. Structella [Castro et al., 2004] replaces the random graph of Gnutella with the structured overlay of Pastry, while retaining the flexible data placement of unstructured P2P overlays. Queries in Structella are propagated using either flooding or random walks. A peer maintains and uses its structured routing table to flood a query to its neighbors, thus ensuring that peers are visited only once during a query and avoiding duplicate messages.

Interest & Locality-based

Foreseer [Cai and Wang, 2004] is a P2P system that combines an interest-aware overlay and a locality-aware overlay. Thus, each peer has two bounded sets of neighbors: proximity-based (called *neighbors*) and interest-based (called *friends*). Finding neighbors relies on a very basic algorithm that improves locality-awareness slowly with time. Whenever a node discovers new peers, it replaces its neighbors with the ones that are closer in latency. A similar scheme is used to progressively make and refine friends from the peers that satisfy queries of the node in question. Friends are preferentially selected by comparing their data similarity with the target node.

Joint Overlay

[Maniymaran et al., 2007] leverages the idea of cohabiting several P2P overlays on a same network, so that the best overlay could be chosen depending on the application. The distinctive feature of this proposal is that, in the joint overlay, the cohabiting overlays share information to reduce their maintenance cost while keeping the same level of performance. As an example, they describe the creation of a joint overlay with a structured overlay and an interest-based unstructured overlay using gossip protocols. Thus, each peer belongs to both overlays and can alternatively use them.

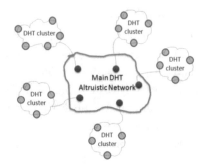

Figure 1.12: A two-layer DHT overlay [Ntarmos and Triantafillou, 2004].

DHT Layering or Hierarchy

A structured overlay [Ntarmos and Triantafillou, 2004] is organized into multiple layers in order to improve performance under high levels of churn. They identify two types of peers: altruistic and selfish. The idea is to concentrate most routing chores at altruistic peers; these peers are willing to carry extra load and have the required capabilities to do so. The authors also assume that altruistic peers stay connected more than others. Thus, a main structured overlay is built over altruistic peers, and each one in its turn is connected to a smaller structured overlay of less altruistic peers. Figure 1.12 shows an example of a two-layer DHT, where the main DHT represents the altruistic network and links several DHT-structured clusters. The P2P overlay can be further clustered, resulting into multiple layers.

A similar work [Shen and Xu, 2008] addresses the problem of load balancing in a heterogenous environment in terms of capacities. Likewise, a main structured overlay is built over high-capacity peers, and each one acts as a super-peer for a locality-based cluster of regular peers. Each peer has an identifier obtained by hashing its locality information (using the binning technique of Section 1.5.1). A regular peer is assigned to a super-peer whose identifier is closest to the peer's identifier, which results in regular peers being connected to their physically closest super-peer.

1.6 CONCLUSION

In this chapter, we first introduced the three main kinds of P2P overlays: unstructured, structured and super-peer. We briefly described each of these P2P overlays, and compared them based on the main requirements for data management: autonomy, query expressiveness, efficiency, quality of service, fault-tolerance and security. Each kind of P2P overlay provides partial support for these requirements. For example, structured overlays have low query expressiveness, super-peer overlays are not fault-tolerant, and unstructured overlays are usually inefficient in query processing.

Then, we presented the techniques for routing queries to relevant peers. We first described the algorithms of query routing in unstructured overlays. The main concern in these overlays is how to route the query to obtain high quality answers while minimizing the communication cost.

Usually, the algorithms where peers maintain some kind of statistics outperform the others. However, for highly dynamic systems, these algorithms may incur a high communication overhead without significant gains in answers' quality. We also discussed the problem of query routing in structured overlays, particularly in DHTs. We presented the main routing geometries that are used in DHTs. We analyzed the routing properties of these geometries and compared them from the point of view of these properties.

Afterwards, we provided generic definition and description of gossip protocols, and investigated the ways P2P systems can leverage these protocols. Then, we focused on the salient strengths and weaknesses of gossip protocols from the point of the view of P2P data management.

Then, we briefly surveyed P2P replication techniques as they can be used to improve data availability in a P2P system.

Finally, we discussed advanced features that can be incorporated in the construction of the P2P overlay and improve the performance of data management techniques. Along these lines, matching the overlay with a locality- or interest-aware scheme could bring great benefits to the P2P system in terms of scalability, efficiency and quality of service. Another feature is the combination of different overlays and schemes, in order to exploit their different advantages.

CHAPTER 2

Content Distribution in P2P Systems

2.1 INTRODUCTION

Given the explosive growth of the Internet, web-servers suffer congestion and bottleneck, which substantially decreases their quality of service [Wang, 1999]. In other terms, the web-server can easily get overwhelmed by the traffic due to a sudden spike in its content popularity. As a result, the website becomes temporarily unavailable or its clients experience long download times, which leaves them in frustration. That is why the World Wide Web is often called World Wide Wait [Mohan, 2001].

In order to improve the Internet service quality, a new technology has emerged that efficiently delivers the web content to large audiences. It is called *Content Distribution Network* or *Content Delivery Network* (CDN) [Buyya et al., 2008]. A commercial CDN like Akamai[1] is a network of dedicated servers that are strategically spread across the Internet and that cooperate to deliver content to end-users. A content provider like Google or CNN can sign up with a CDN so that its content is deployed over the servers of the CDN. Then, the requests for the deployed content are transparently redirected to and handled by the CDN on behalf of the original web-servers. As a result, CDNs decrease the workload on the web-servers, reduce bandwidth costs, and lower the user-perceived latency. In short, CDNs strike a balance between the costs incurred on content providers and the QoS provided to the users [Pallis and Vakali, 2006]. CDNs have become a huge market for generating large revenues since they provide content providers with the highly required *scalabiliy, reliability,* and *performance*. However, CDN services are quite expensive, often out of reach for small enterprises or non-profit organizations.

P2P systems that deal with content sharing (e.g., sharing files or web documents) can be seen as a form of CDN, where peers share content and deliver it on each other's behalf [Saroiu et al., 2002]. The more popular the content (e.g., file or web-page), the more available it becomes as more peers download it and eventually provide it for others. Thus, the P2P model is a low-cost alternative to traditional CDNs like Akamai when handling increasing amounts of users and demands. Whereas a CDN must invest more in its infrastructure by adding servers, new users bring their own resources into a P2P system. This implies that P2P systems are a perfect match for building cheap and scalable CDN infrastructures. However, making use of P2P self-scalability is not a straightforward endeavor because designing an efficient P2P system is very challenging.

---

[1]http://www.akamai.com. Accessed on December 2011

This chapter reviews the state-of-the-art for both traditional and P2P content distribution in order to identify the shortcomings and highlight the challenges. It is organized as follows. In Section 2.2, we give more insight into traditional CDNs and the requirements which are needed for the design of novel and cheaper alternatives. Then, in Section 2.3, we deeply explore P2P solutions for content distribution. We evaluate the existing approaches against the previously identified requirements and show open issues.

2.2   INSIGHTS ON TRADITIONAL CONTENT DISTRIBUTION

Content distribution networks are an important web caching application. First, let us briefly review the different web caching techniques in order to position and understand the CDN technology. Then, we focus on CDNs, their requirements and their open issues.

2.2.1   BACKGROUND ON WEB CACHING

A web cache is a disk storage of predefined size that is reserved for content requested from the Internet (such as HTML pages and images)[2]. After an original request for an object has been successfully fulfilled, and that object has been stored in the cache, further requests for this object result in returning it from the cache rather than the web-server. The cache content is temporary as the objects are dynamically cached and discarded according to predefined policies. When the cache is full, the LRU policy, for instance, replaces the least recently used object with the new object .

Web caching is widely acknowledged as providing three major advantages. First, it reduces the bandwidth consumption since fewer requests and responses need to go over the network. Second, it reduces the load on the web-server which handles fewer requests. Third, it reduces the user-perceived latency since a cached request is served from the web cache (which is closer to the client) instead of the original web-server. Together, these advantages make the web less expensive and better performing.

Web caching can be implemented at various locations using *proxy servers* [Mohan, 2001, Wang, 1999]. A *proxy server* acts as an intermediary for requests from clients to web-servers. It intercepts each request, and either serves the requested web-page from its cache or redirects the request to the web-server. A proxy server can be placed in the user's local computer as part of its web browser or at various points between the user and the web-servers. Commonly, proxy caching refers to the latter schemes that involve dedicated servers out on the network while the user's local proxy cache is rather known as *browser cache*.

Depending on their placement and their usage purpose, we distinguish two kinds of proxies: *forward proxies* and *reverse proxies*. They are illustrated in Figure 2.1.

A *forward proxy* is used as a gateway between an organisation (i.e., a group of clients) and the Internet. It makes requests on behalf of the clients of the organisation. Then, it caches requested

---

[2]Web caching is different from traditional caching in main memory that aims at limiting disk accesses.

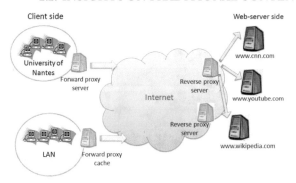

Figure 2.1: Web caching: different locations for proxy servers.

objects to serve subsequent requests coming from other clients of the organisation. Large corporations and Internet Service Providers (ISP) often set up forward proxies on their firewalls to reduce their bandwidth costs by filtering out repeated requests. As illustrated in Figure 2.1, the university of Nantes has deployed a forward proxy that interacts with the Internet on behalf of the university users and handles their queries.

A *reverse proxy* is used in a network in front of web-servers. It is delegated the authority to operate on behalf of these web-servers, while working in close cooperation with them. Typically, all requests addressed to one of the web-servers are routed through the proxy server which tries to serve them via caching. Figure 2.1 shows a reverse proxy that acts on behalf of the web-servers of wikipedia.com, cnn.com, and youtube.com by handling their received queries. A CDN deploys reverse proxies throughout the Internet and sells caching to websites that aim for larger audience and lower workload. The reverse proxies of a CDN are commonly known as *surrogate servers*.

2.2.2   OVERVIEW OF CDN

A CDN deploys hundreds of surrogate servers around the globe. The servers store the content of different web-servers and therefore handle related queries on behalf of these web-servers. Each website selects specific or popular content (e.g., HTML pages, images, audio, and video files) and pushes it to the CDN. The CDN manages the replication and/or caching of the content among its surrogate servers. Clients requesting this content are then redirected to their closest surrogate server. Figure 2.2 gives an overview of a CDN that distributes and delivers the content of a web-server in the US. The figure shows how queries are treated based on the localities of the clients.

2.2.3   REQUIREMENTS AND OPEN ISSUES OF CDN

As introduced previously, a CDN network has to fulfill important requirements which are mainly *reliability*, *performance*, and *scalability* [Pallis and Vakali, 2006].

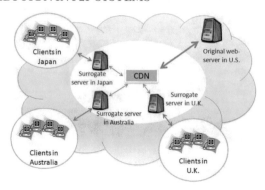

Figure 2.2: Overview of a CDN.

- **Reliability** guarantees that a client can always find and access its desired content. For this, the network should be robust and avoid single point of failure (i.e., SOP).

- **Performance** mainly involves the response time perceived by end-users submitting queries. Slow response time is the single greatest contributor to clients abandoning websites [Technologies, 2004].

- **Scalability** refers to the adaptability of the network to handle more amounts of content, users and requests without significant decline in performance. For this, the network should prevent bottlenecks due to overload situations.

The reliability and performance of a CDN are highly affected by the mechanisms of content distribution as well as content location and query routing. Content distribution defines how the content is distributed over the CDN and made available for clients. It mainly deals with the placement of content and involves caching and replication techniques in order to make the same content accessible from several locations. Thus, with these techniques, the content is located near to the clients yielding low response times and high content availability since many replicas are distributed. Content location and routing defines how to locate the requested content and route requests towards the appropriate and relevant servers.

To expand and scale-up, CDNs need to invest significant time and costs in provisioning additional infrastructures (e.g., more servers) [Technologies, 2004]. Otherwise, they would compromise the quality of service received by individual clients. Further, they should dynamically adapt their resource provisioning in order to address unexpected and varying workloads. This inevitably leads to more expensive services for websites. In the near future, the clients will also have to pay to receive high-quality content (in some of today's websites like CNN.com, users have already started to pay a subscription to view videos). In this context, scalability is to deliver high-quality content while maintaining low operational costs [Buyya et al., 2008].

Most recently, traditional CDNs [Buyya et al., 2008] have turned towards P2P technology to reduce investments in their own infrastructure, in the context of video streaming. The key idea is to dynamically couple traditional CDN distribution with P2P distribution. Basically, the CDN serves a handful of clients which in turn provide the content to other clients. Joost[3] and BitTorrent[4] are today's most representative CDN companies using P2P technology to deliver Internet television and video streaming, respectively.

To conclude this section, we observe that P2P technology is being progressively accepted and adopted as a means of content distribution. The existing CDNs still depend—at least partly—on a dedicated infrastructure, which requires investment and centralized administration. If the CDN could rely on a cheap P2P infrastructure supported only by end-users, this would provide a cheap and scalable alternative. In the rest of this chapter, we further investigate the feasibility of pure P2P content distribution.

2.3   P2P CONTENT DISTRIBUTION

Most of the current P2P applications fall within the category of content distribution, which range from simple file sharing, to more sophisticated systems that create a distributed overlay for organizing, indexing, searching and retrieving content [Androutsellis-Theotokis and Spinellis, 2004b]. P2P content distribution functionality is achieved via collaboration among a large scale of peers, scalability is ensured by resource sharing (content, storage, bandwidth, etc.). Therefore, by distributing tasks across all participating peers, they can collectively carry out large-scale content distribution without the need for powerful and dedicated servers.

2.3.1   ADVANCED FEATURES USED BY LARGE-SCALE P2P CDN

In Chapter 1, we identified advanced features that can be used to refine the P2P overlay and hence improve the performance of the P2P application. These features basically consist in incorporating locality- or interest-awareness into the P2P overlay, and combining multiple overlays. When exploiting these features for large-scale content distribution, one should make sure that the overhead is worth the performance improvement.

One of the major challenges is to capture the information, whether topological or semantically, in a manner that is both practical and scalable. This should be done without requiring global knowledge or centralized administration or incurring large overheads of messages and/or data transfers on the P2P CDN.

Another challenge is to avoid grouping peers into a static configuration which does not evolve well as the interests, localities, or behaviors of peers change. Indeed, this might severely affect the quality of service of the P2P CDN, with respect to content search and download.

---

[3]http://www.joost.com. Accessed on December 2011
[4]The technology is called *BitTorrent DNA* (*Delivery Network Accelerator*). Available at http://www.bittorrent.com/dna/. Accessed on December 2011.

Locality Awareness

The performance requirement of a CDN cannot be achieved unless content location and query routing mechanisms are locality-aware. Indeed, a CDN has a duty to quickly locate copies of the requested content that are close to the client in locality. While many P2P systems abstract any topological information about the underlying network, locality-awareness should be a top priority in a P2P CDN.

When a peer has close-by contacts, it can first query them or (even better) download content from them before communicating with randomly located peers. Hence, locality-aware solutions greatly contribute in reducing communication and data transfer costs, which in turn improves the user-perceived latency.

However, as laid out previously, these solution should be kept simple, incur acceptable overhead, operate fast and adapt to dynamicity and high scales.

Interest Awareness

Most P2P approaches tend to sacrifice autonomy to achieve efficiency [Daswani et al., 2003]. This is because less autonomy allows more control on the content placement and topology such that there exist a deterministic way to locate content within bounded cost.

Nevertheless, it might be useful to leverage the interests of peers in a P2P CDN to implement intelligent mechanisms and at the same time respect their autonomy.

Instead of forcing peers to replicate undesired content, an interesting alternative is to elaborate on the natural replication of content whereby peers replicate the content they request as they download them.

Leveraging interests of peers to organize them can greatly improve the efficiency of content search. Peer A that shares the same interests as peer B, is likely to have already downloaded content that might be requested by peer B. Thus, it might be useful to establish a connection between A and B. However, since a peer's interests might change with time, the interest-based scheme must be able to detect changes and accordingly adapt.

P2P Overlay Combination

As mentioned in Chapter 1, structured and unstructured overlays should not be seen as competing but rather complementing each other. Each category provides specific and unique functionalities.

In unstructured overlays, the freedom in content placement provides maximum flexibility in selecting policies for replication and caching. Furthermore, content popularity derives a kind of natural replication among peers, which induces high availability. Indeed, peers replicate the content they request upon download.

In opposition, structured overlays are the perfect match for a P2P CDN that seeks a scalable and guaranteed lookup but does not witness highly dynamic populations.

Thus, combining different overlays in a P2P CDN might reveal interesting, yet very challenging. In particular, the maintenance of several overlays should not overwhelm the P2P CDN or limit its scalability. An interesting solution is to leverage the combination in the maintenance mechanisms (e.g., exploiting one overlay to maintain the other).

2.3.2   P2P CDN SOLUTIONS

Several P2P approaches have been proposed to distribute web content over P2P overlays in order to relieve the original web servers. These use the P2P overlays discussed earlier (e.g., hybrid, unstructured, DHT-based).

To the best of our knowledge, the P2P CDNs that are currently available for public use mainly comprise CoralCDN [Freedman et al., 2004], CoDeeN [Pai et al., 2004], and CobWeb [Song et al., 2005]. These systems are deployed over PlanetLab which provides a relatively trusted environment consisting of nodes donated largely by the research community. Basically, they rely on a network of cooperative reverse proxy servers that distribute web content and handle related queries. Such systems cannot be categorized as pure P2P solutions because they are using dedicated servers rather than exploiting client resources. The only P2P characteristic exhibited by these systems is the absence of centralized administration. We examine one typical example of these systems, CoralCDN.

CoralCDN [Freedman et al., 2004] relies on a hierarchy of tree-based overlays that cluster nearby nodes. Each level of the hierarchy consists of several overlays, and each overlay consists of the set of nodes whose average pair-wise RTTs are below the threshold defined by this level. A node is member of one overlay at each hierarchy level and retains the same node identifier in all overlays to which it belongs. Figure 2.3 illustrates a three-level hierarchy with RTT thresholds of ∞, 60 ms, and 20 ms for level 0, 1, and 2, respectively. It focuses on Node R and only shows the three overlays to which R belongs at each level. R is physically the closest to C_2 among the nodes (C_0, C_1, C_2, C_3) because R and C_2 share the highest-level overlay.

Each overlay is structured according to a tree as shown in Figure 2.3. A key is mapped to several nodes whose IDs are numerically close to the key, in order to avoid hot spots [5]. A node stores pointers related to the object whose key is mapped to its node identifier. In Figure 2.3, Node R has the same node identifier in all its overlays; we can view a node as projecting its presence to the same logical location in each of its overlays.

Based on this indexing hierarchy, CoralCDN allows to locate web object copies hosted by nearby proxies of CoralCDN: the proxies will be represented by the nodes of the hierarchy. Based on its RTT measurements, a client is redirected via the DNS services to a nearby CoralCDN proxy which eventually provides her the requested object. If not cached locally, the proxy can perform a key-based routing throughout its overlays in order to find a pointer to a remote copy of the object; it starts at the highest-level overlay of the proxy to benefit from network locality then progresses down the hierarchy. Once the object is fetched and locally cached, the proxy inserts pointers to itself, with respect to the object, in the different overlays to which belongs this proxy: it stores at each node responsible for this object its own address information along with the object identifier.

---

[5]A node becomes a hot spot when it stores a popular content and gets overloaded by requests for this object.

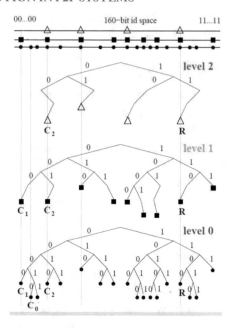

Figure 2.3: CoralCDN hierarchy of key-based overlays [Freedman et al., 2004].

Centralized Approaches

The first category of approaches [Padmanabhan and Sripanidkulchai, 2002, Ryu and Yang, 2005] relies on the web-server that centralizes and manages the directory information. Basically, the server maintains a directory of peers to which its objects have been transferred in the past and manages the redirection of queries. When a client queries for an object, the server returns the addresses of several peers from its redirection directory. The client first tries to retrieve the object from one of those peers. If this fails, the object is directly served by the server.

To minimize redirection failures in a P2P dynamic environment, OLP [Ryu and Yang, 2005] tries to predict the object lifetime and accordingly selects the peer to which the query should be redirected. However, redirection in OLP does not consider locality-awareness when providing clients with object locations. CoopNet [Padmanabhan and Sripanidkulchai, 2002] tries to incorporate locality-awareness as the web-server sends to the requester client a list of nearby peers that can provide the requested object. To limit the server redirection, a client connects to the peers indicated by the web-server and forms a small network with them. However, there is no well-defined query routing algorithms within these networks. Moreover, CoopNet does not deal with dynamic aspects because the web-server cannot detect which peers in its directory have failed or discarded their cached objects.

Centralized approaches lack robustness, because whenever the web-server fails, its content is no longer accessible in spite of available peers with cached copies. As with the traditional server/client model, the server is still a single point of failure (i.e., SPOF). Scaling such systems requires replacing the web server with a more powerful one, to be able to redirect the queries of a large audience.

Unstructured Approaches

The second category of approaches uses unstructured overlays for their flexibility and inherent robustness. Two representative systems are Proofs and BuddyWeb.

- **Proofs** [Stavrou et al., 2002]. Uses an unstructured overlay in which peers continuously exchange neighbors among each other like in gossip protocols. This provides each peer with a random view of the system for each query routing operation. Peers keep their requested objects and can then provide them to other participants. To locate one of the object replicas, a query is flooded to a random subset of neighbors with a fixed TTL, i.e., the max number of hops. The continuous randomization of the overlay has the benefit of improving the network fault-tolerance and tends to uniformly distribute the load over peers. However, the blind searches for not not-so popular objects induce heavy traffic overheads and high latencies. Moreover, Proofs does not address locality-awareness which is useful to forward queries to close results.

- **BuddyWeb** [Wang et al., 2002]. It also uses an unstructured network and flooding for query routing. Notice that central servers provide each newly joining peer with neighbors that share interest similarities with the peer. However, these servers can present single points of failures (i.e., SPOF), which makes BuddyWeb vulnerable and limits its scalability. Similar to Proofs, BuddyWeb does not take into account locality-awareness.

Structured Approaches

Now, we examine existing approaches that rely on structured overlays in order to benefit from their efficient lookup. First, we examine Squirrel [Iyer et al., 2002], PoPCache [Rao et al., 2007], and Backslash [Stading et al., 2002] which propose 2 types of strategies: *DHT-Home* and *DHT-Directory*. Then, we discuss different approaches.

DHT-Home Strategy places objects at peers with the numerically closest identifier with respect to the hash of the URL of the object without any locality or interest considerations (see Figure 2.4 (b)). Queries find the peer that has the object by navigating through the DHT. To deal with highly popular objects, objects may be progressively replicated along neighbors as the number of requests increases. This is achieved by further forcing peers to store arbitrary content.

DHT-Directory Strategy stores at the peer identified by the hash of the object's URL a small directory of pointers to recent downloaders of the object (see Figure 2.4 (a)). A query first navigates through the DHT and then receives a pointer to a peer that potentially has the object. Approaches adopting this strategy may be vulnerable since the directory information is abruptly lost in case of failures.

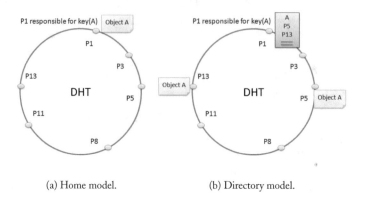

(a) Home model.   (b) Directory model.

Figure 2.4: DHT strategies in a P2P CDN.

In general, such systems are self-scalable because of the DHT load balancing and replication mechanisms. However, there are two main drawbacks in the query routing with respect to the requirement of CDNs on short latencies. First, each query has to navigate through the whole DHT, which implies several routing hops. This can be acceptable in corporate LAN environments, where the latency of the network links are a magnitude smaller than the latency of the server. Otherwise, the server will be much faster. Second, unless using a locality-aware overlay combined with proactive replication, the query is randomly served by any peer.

Joint-Overlay Approaches

Kache [Linga et al., 2003] relies on a new form of DHT that increases robustness by increasing memory usage and communication overhead. Using a hash function, peers are organized into $\sqrt{N}$ groups, where N = total number of peers. This is shown in Figure 2.5 with focus on the peer with identifier 110 from group 0. The peer maintains (a) a view of its own group (i.e., peers 30 and 160), and (b) for each foreign group, a small (constant-sized) set of contact peers lying in it (i.e., peer 432). Each entry (group view or contact) carries additional fields such as RTT estimates. Peer 110 also stores directory information related to each single object that is cached in the system and whose URL maps to group 0 by means of hashing. For each such object o, peer 110 has a *directory table* that contains the IP addresses of a bounded set of peers holding a copy of o.

When a peer p downloads a copy of the object o, it creates a directory entry $< o, p >$ and communicates it to each contact c that belongs to o's group. When the directory table of peer c is full, c performs RTT measurements to keep the directory entries that refer to the closest peers and discard the other entries. Each peer gossips within its group to replicate and spread directory entries; it selects close-by peers from its view to exchange gossip messages. Obviously, peers gossiping and replicating directory entries are not necessarily interested in this information. Furthermore, since

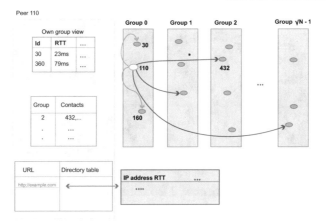

Figure 2.5:   A Kache system with peers distributed across $\sqrt{N}$ groups, and soft state at a typical peer [Linga et al., 2003].

directory information is highly replicated, vast updates are required when referenced peers discard their content or leave the network.

Kache is robust against failures, because all peers in the same group store pointers of all the objects mapped onto the group. Moreover, locality-awareness is incorporated through the RTT-based routing tables. Lookups are bounded by $O(1)$, thus scaling does not influence lookup time. However, the resources necessary to maintain routing information increase as the number of peers increases.

Flower-CDN [Dick et al., 2009] supports several under-provisioned websites with large user-base, by strictly relying on their user communities rather than dedicated and reliable servers. Figure 2.6 illustrates the architecture of Flower-CDN. Participant peers belonging to the same lo-

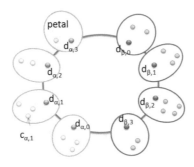

Figure 2.6:   Flower-CDN architecture with websites α and β and four localities.

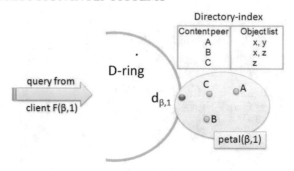

Figure 2.7: Query submitted by F, a new client of β in locality $loc = 1$.

cality loc and interested in the same website ws build together an unstructured overlay noted **petal**(ws, loc), using gossip protocols. These peers, called *content peers* and noted $c_{ws,loc}$, cache and provide content of ws, thus considerably relieving the server of ws from its query load. Within a petal, peers use gossip protocols to exchange information about their content and contacts, allowing Flower-CDN to maintain accurate information despite dynamic changes in order to support eventual queries. Flower-CDN charges one peer of each *petal*(ws, loc), the role of a *directory peer* (noted $d_{ws,loc}$): $d_{ws,loc}$ knows all content peers $c_{ws,loc}$ and keeps a directory about their stored content. Directory peers connect via **D-ring**, a DHT-based structured overlay, to handle queries coming from new clients. D-ring relies on a locality- and interest-aware key service that assigns each directory peer an identifier based on the website and locality it represents.

Instead of querying server ws, a new client located in loc, submits its query to D-ring which transfers the query to the directory peer in charge of ws in loc i.e., $d_{ws,loc}$. Then, $d_{ws,loc}$ tries to resolve the query while relying on its petal or some neighboring petals related to ws. Figure 2.7 shows a part of D-ring and focuses on the directory peer $d_{\beta,1}$ and three content peers for $(\beta, 1)$, namely A, B and C. $d_{\beta,1}$ maintains a directory-index that lists, for each peer in *petal*$(\beta, 1)$, their objects (e.g., A holds objects x and y which are initially provided by website β). Moreover, $d_{\beta,1}$ stores directory summaries received from its direct neighbors, i.e., $d_{\beta,0}$ and $d_{\beta,2}$. Assume that a new client F of website β enters the system with a query q for some object x. Supposing that client F is located in $loc = 1$, q is forwarded to $d_{\beta,1}$ which searches its directory index for x. Then, $d_{\beta,1}$ redirects q to content peer A or C, which hold a copy of x and thus can serve the query. A or C directly transfer the object to the client to F.

In case the client F has requested object x' which is not held by any peer in *petal*$(\beta, 1)$, $d_{\beta,1}$ first checks its directory summaries for $(\beta, 0)$ and $(\beta, 2)$ to see if they might have x' in their directory index. If it appears so, $d_{\beta,1}$ forwards q accordingly to either $d_{\beta,0}$ or $d_{\beta,2}$. Otherwise, the client F redirects q to the website β.

Afterwards, the client F can join *petal*$(\beta, 1)$ as a content peer $c_{\beta,1}$. Initially, F gets to know from $d_{\beta,1}$ content peers like A. F gossips to A to discover other content peers in its petal and to

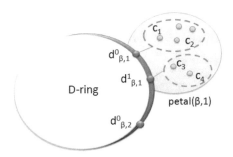

Figure 2.8: Example of *petal*(β, 1) in PetalUp-CDN.

get updates about their shared content. Therefore, for further queries, F searches directly in its *petal*(β, 1) instead of relying on D-ring.

PetalUp-CDN [Dick et al., 2011] addresses the scalability and robustness of Flower-CDN. PetalUp-CDN allows several directory peers to share the management of the same petal. Directory peers for each couple (ws, loc) consecutively join D-ring. The number of directory peers in charge of each *petal*(ws, loc) increases progressively as the number of clients for ws in loc increases. By having multiple directory peers in charge of a petal, the failure of one or more of these directory peers will not lead to a complete loss of directory information, and will allow the system to continue in a slightly-reduced capacity. Moreover, these additional directory peers are not carrying redundant information, but each one is responsible for maintaining information about a part of the petal. An example of PetalUp-CDN configuration is illustrated in Figure 2.8 which focuses on *petal*(β, 1). Two directory peers $d_{\beta,1}^0$ and $d_{\beta,1}^1$ share the management of *petal*(β, 1). Thus, they each manage a subset of the content peers $c_{\beta,1}$.

The petals expand progressively as new peers join and shrink as existing ones leave. To keep the load on directory peers at bay, D-ring follows the evolution of the petals and accordingly may automatically expand or shrink. Failures and disconnections are detected and recovered via gossip protocols. Gossiping is confined in petals, or in other terms localities, which yields acceptable overhead in terms of bandwidth consumption and reduced latency.

Discussion

Table 2.1 summarizes the performance behavior of the P2P CDN approaches previously described. An important observation is that most of the approaches do not focus on scalability, and often target small local networks.

In CoralCDN, users are not involved in the P2P network: they use the P2P CDN but do not contribute and share their resources. An increase of the number of users requires more investment by adding proxy caches to the CoralCDN. OLP is unsuitable for P2P systems as it is not scalable (i.e.,

System	Overlay	Robustness	Scalability	Locality	Autonomy
		Table 2.1: Comparison of P2P networks			
CoralCDN	hierarchy of proxies	yes	proxy investment	yes	–
OLP	centralized	SPOF	server bottleneck	no	yes
CoopNet	centralized	SPOF	server bottleneck	no	yes
Proof	unstructured	randomness	flooding overhead	no	yes
BuddyWeb	unstructured	SPOF	server bottleneck	no	yes
DHT-Directory	structured	directory loss	yes	no	yes
DHT-Home	structured	DHT	yes	no	no
Kache	joint overlay	replication	overhead	yes	yes
Flower-CDN	joint overlay	gossip	no	yes	yes
PetalUp-CDN	joint overlay	gossip	yes	yes	yes

bottlenecks) nor robust (i.e., SPOF) due to its centralized nature, and it does not address locality-awareness. CoopNet has similar limitations, except that it supports locality-aware redirection of queries. Proof derives its robustness from the randomness of unstructured overlays, but in return suffers from their scalability issues due to flooding overhead and lacks locality-awareness. BuddyWeb does not cope with dynamic and large-scale participation of peers because its construction mechanism is centralized, and thus is not adapted for real P2P environments. DHT-Directory approaches do not provide robustness as the performance of query handling is directly affected by peer failures. In comparison, DHT-Home approaches rely on DHT robustness which incurs high maintenance costs and breaks the autonomy of peers due to its replication mechanism. Kache addresses most of the requirements, and most importantly achieves robustness by replicating and gossiping indexing information. However, Kache's scalability comes at the cost of a significant storage overhead on every peer. PetalUp-CDN is designed to achieve scalability at low costs while respecting peer autonomy and complying with peer localities.

2.4   CONCLUSION

The objective of this chapter was to provide a concise, yet comprehensive study of P2P content distribution.

After a first overview of traditional CDNs, we identified their requirements which are performance, scalability, and reliability, and we discussed the mechanisms needed to fulfill each requirement. We focused on the potential savings and benefits in using P2P technology as a cheap and efficient alternative for commercial CDNs.

We then presented the recent P2P trends that can improve the performance of P2P content distribution but incur additional challenges. The trends that we identified are locality-aware and interest-aware overlay matching, and overlay combination. The challenges are to keep the solutions simple, avoid centralized management and large overheads, operate fast and dynamically adapt to changes and massive scales.

Finally, we focused on P2P CDN which have stringent performance requirements. They should be highly robust, efficient, and scalable, while taking into account the autonomy of peers. Existing P2P CDNs do not answer all the important requirements. Most importantly, they are not designed to achieve high scalability as they target small scales.

CHAPTER 3

Recommendation Systems

The explosive growth of web-scale collaboration has increased the amount of information that is available to users. Therefore, people use a variety of strategies to search for contents and make choices about what to explore. Recommendation systems have emerged as software applications that help users to make choices. Recommendation systems have roots in information retrieval (IR). IR deals with searching for the contents that match a given query, and then retrieve those contents to the users. IR systems typically return a large number of responses that are related to a given query. Thus, users get overwhelmed and it becomes hard for them to find the most valuable and relevant contents.

In this chapter, we are concerned with recommendation for decentralized infrastructures where users wish to keep their contents (documents, items, images, tables, etc.) in their own workspace, which is typically the case for on-line communities [Cheng and Vassileva, 2005]. An on-line community refers to a information system where anyone can post content. In this chapter, we consider on-line communities such as researchers or friends who wish to share data and want to keep their data in their own workspace instead of storing it in an unknown server. In this context, P2P is appropriate to handle content sharing as the underlying infrastructure. P2P file-sharing systems have proven to be very efficient at locating content given specific queries. However, file-sharing systems only provide a very simple keyword search capability, trying to find the contents whose name or description match the keywords provided by the user. Few solutions exist that are able to recommend the most relevant files. Recently, a significant amount of effort has been given to introduce recommendation to suggest the most relevant contents.

The goal of this chapter is to show how different P2P techniques may be useful for decentralizing recommendation mostly for on-line communities. We present the basis of recommendation and afterwards we classify the most relevant P2P recommendation solutions. Aberer [2010] lecture presents interesting recommendation models for Web page retrieval based on data mining techniques. The focus is on how to discover and model users' interest in order to recommend related web pages. Notice that the context is different from ours since they are not concerned with on-line communities.

This chapter is organized as follows. In Section 3.1, we present and discuss the main concepts related to centralized recommendation systems: collaborative filtering, content-based filtering and social networks. Next, in Section 3.2, we present the most relevant P2P solutions related to P2P content management systems as they come with interesting techniques that may be exploited for P2P recommendation. In Section 3.3, we describe the most important approaches for P2P recommendation. Finally, in Section 3.4, we summarize and conclude the chapter by proposing a general framework for recommendation.

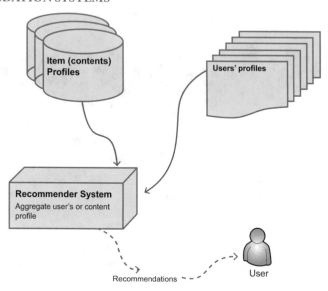

Figure 3.1: Overview of Recommendation Systems.

3.1   OVERVIEW OF RECOMMENDATION

Recommendation Systems (RS) are software applications that analyze users' historical patterns (ratings, purchases, preferences, etc.) to find and recommend new items that the user might be interested in and would like to explore or purchase [Resnick and Varian, 1997]. Figure 3.1 provides a general overview of a recommendation system and its main components. In general, an RS first collects a users' historical patterns that may be expressed either explicitly or implicitly. Historical patterns allow to capture user profiles or user preferences. They may include information about a user (such as name, age, location, etc.), or users' activity history (what the user bought, viewed, rated, etc.), or description of the items the user has seen, purchased, explored or rated. After exploiting a user pattern, the RS finds and aggregates other users with similar patterns. Finally, the RS uses the data from those similar users to suggest items the user might be interested in. In this chapter, depending on the context, we use alternatively the term item, content or document to refer to a general content.

There are two main kinds of RSs [Goldberg et al., 1992, Malone et al., 1987, McLaughlin and Herlocker, 2004, Ziegler et al., 2005,?]: collaborative filtering (CF) and content-based filtering. CFs can recommend items based on the items previously rated by similar users. Content-based RSs work by suggesting to the user items that are similar to items the user has seen or rated [Breese et al., 1998]. Finally, social network links can also be exploited as a recommendation approach in which friendship is taken into account to increase the quality of recommendation. In the next following subsections, we review each approach.

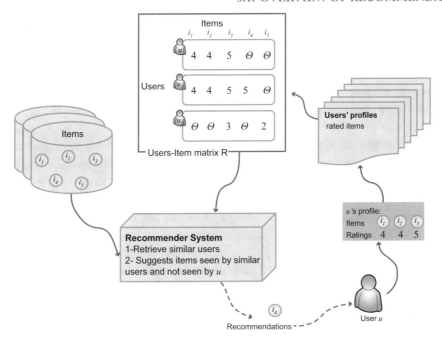

Figure 3.2: Collaborative Filtering.

3.1.1   COLLABORATIVE FILTERING

CF is one of the most popular classes of recommendation algorithms. CF systems try to automate the process of word-of-mouth, whereby people who have the same preferences most probably have similar taste and interest. In CF systems, users express their preferences by rating items (photos, documents, etc.) either explicitly or implicitly. The user ratings, are often represented by discrete values within a certain range, e.g., between 1 and 5, higher meaning better.

CF has been widely used for building RSs [Resnick et al., 1994], Ringo/Firefly [Shardanand and Maes, 1995], and Tapestry RS [Goldberg et al., 1992]. It works by measuring the similarity between users based on their rating behavior. Two users are similar if they rate items in a similar way (the ratings values are close enough). CF typically works in four steps.

1. Measure the similarity between user u and all the other users in the system.

2. Select those users who are most similar to u, noted $neighbors(u)$.

3. Normalize and compute the weighted sum of the $neighbors(u)$ ratings.

4. Make recommendations based on those ratings, using *top-k* algorithms (see Chapter 4).

In CF systems, user profiles are managed through a $U \times I$ user-item matrix R, as shown in Figure 3.2, where U represents the set of users and I the set of items in the system. In addition, n is the number of users and m the number of items. Each entry $r_{u,i}$ of R includes the rating given by user u for item i, where $r_{u,i} = r$ indicates that user u rated item i by a value of r, and $r_{u,i} = \ddot{\text{i}}\dagger\Phi$ indicates that user u did not rate item i yet. Each row $r_u \in R$ is a user profile that corresponds to the items rated by u. Data sparsity (missing rates in the user-item matrix) is a well common phenomena in CF. Thus, another goal of the CF system is to predict missing rates in matrix R. Notice that due to the size of R, the storage and management of inverted lists used to provide recommendation is known to be prohibitive space-wise for a single server [Amer-Yahia et al., 2008].

The *neighborhood* of a user u is defined as the most similar users among all users. Thus, a similarity measure is necessary. One popular measure is *cosine similarity* [Linden et al., 2003, Sarwar et al., 2001]: the similarity between a user u and another user v, noted $sim(u, v)$, is computed by making the product between the ratings that was given by u and v over their items. Another known similarity measure is the *Pearson correlation coefficients* [Massa and Avesani, 2004, Sarwar et al., 2001]. It was first introduced into collaborative filtering as a weighting method in the GroupLens project [Resnick et al., 1994].

Collaborative filtering systems have proven very successful for recommendation in many e-commerce applications. However, CF suffers from several drawbacks.

- **Data sparsity**. Most users rate small numbers of items in the system, thus making it hard to find similar users and perform rate prediction [Linden et al., 2003].

- **Cold start**. A new user who has not yet rated any item will not have similar users to provide with recommendations. On the other hand, when a new item is introduced in the system and no user has rated that item yet, it is not possible to recommend that item [Schein et al., 2002].

- **Privacy**. Users give full control of their behavior and shared items (photos, documents, etc.) to the application provider who can sell it to other and worse, leave such control to third parties of unknown affiliations [Canny, 2002].

- **Limited Scalability**. Measuring the similarity between users is space and time consuming, and increases exponentially as the numbers of items and users increase. This is a major concern for e-commerce applications which provide a lot of recommendations while serving millions of users.

3.1.2   CONTENT-BASED FILTERING

Unlike CF, content-based filtering works by suggesting items that are similar to those that the user has seen or rated. In content-based filtering, the similarity is computed between the items the user has seen or rated and the items that the user did not see or rate yet. Items with high similarity are recommended to the user. Notice that here the user profile is defined based on the semantics of the item the user has seen or rated.

To measure the similarity between items, each item is identified by a set of features and attributes that are usually extracted from its content or description. Therefore, content-based filtering systems are designed mostly to recommend text-based items, or items that have text descriptions (keywords). For instance, the Fab system [Balabanovic and Shoham, 1997] (for web page recommendation) represents a web page by identifying the 100 most important keywords of a page. Similarly, the Webert system [Pazzani and Billsus, 1997] represents documents by identifying the 128 most informative words.

The profile of item i is represented by a vector of keywords, denoted $V_i = \{w_{i,1}, w_{i,2}, ..., w_{i,k}\}$, where k is the total number of unique keywords and $w_{i,j}$ is the weight (importance) of keyword j of item i. One of the popular metrics used to compute the weight $w_{i,j}$ of a keyword j in an item i, is the normalized TF-IDF metric which measures the weight of each keyword by taking into account (in a normalized way) the number of times the most frequent keyword appears in the item, the total amount of items that contains the keyword j and the total amount of items perceived by the user (rated, visited items, user purchases). Notice that a user profile can be represented by a matrix where each row represents an item vector of keywords and includes each weight $w_{i,j}$ defined above.

Users and item profiles may also be extracted using a topic classifier based on machine learning techniques such as LDA (Latent Dirichlet Allocation) [Blei et al., 2003]. These techniques take as input a set of items, and produce as output hidden topics (topics of interest). These extracted topics are used to express both users and items profiles through topic vectors. Again, a user profile can be represented by a matrix. Thus, once users and items profiles are computed, similarity computation is possible. There are several known techniques to evaluate the similarity between these vectors (e.g., user profile and item profile) such as vector-space model, probabilistic models, and fuzzy set models [Pazzani and Billsus, 1997]. As an alternative to machine learning, data mining algorithms may also be used to discover and model user's interests. Gündüz-Ögüdücü [2010] present a complete lecture in this topic.

Once the profiles are defined (keyword or topic vector of rated items), the similarity of user u profile and all items that u did not see or rate is computed. Afterwards, the most similar items are chosen, and rate prediction is done for the items that were not rated yet. Finally, the most similar and high-rate items are recommended. Notice that similarity computation can be quite space and time consuming because it may involve the manipulation of huge matrices.

In addition to the drawbacks found in collaborative filtering, content-based filtering also suffers from **overspecialization**: a user is limited to receive recommendation for items that are only similar to the items she has seen or rated, and thus might not explore new interesting contents.

3.1.3   SOCIAL NETWORKS

Social networks (SN) have become very popular in the context of Web. They allow anybody to present themselves through a profile, and allow them to create, edit, annotate, and share data with other users. The user maintains links to other users, which indicates trust, friendship or shared interests. An SN can be modeled as a graph, where nodes represent users, and an edge between two nodes refers to the relationship between them. In practice, an edge can refer to any type of relationship, e.g., family, friends, common interest, etc. SN exhibits the small-world phenomena, that is, a user

u can contact any other user v in the system in a few hops. Therefore, SNs give users the ability to find new users with similar interests, and locate content in an efficient way.

Social network links and data can be exploited to improve the quality of recommendation results [Shepitsen et al., 2008, Tso-Sutter et al., 2008]. Two main concepts are exploited for recommendation: *trust* and *tagging* . For instance, in order to overcome the cold start problem, the neighbors of each user u may be selected based on the trust network. In this case, each user u computes the trust value between itself and each user in the system. Then, the top-k trustful users are chosen as the neighbors of u.

User tagging activities may also be exploited to enhance recommendation quality [Shepitsen et al., 2008, Tso-Sutter et al., 2008]. A tag is a shared metadata assigned by users to items they have seen or explored, in order to annotate and categorize those items and facilitate item sharing. Tags can also be seen as a kind of index. Tagging activities are commonly used to measure the similarity between users. These systems are known as *Collaborative Tagging*. That is, the fact that users tag the same items is taken into account for similarity computation. In addition, like in content-based filtering, tag contents may be useful to capture the similarity between items.

Amer-Yahia and Yu [2009] describe an interesting and generic system, called community-driven information exploration, that leverages SocialScope [Amer-Yahia et al., 2009b] architecture and Jelly language [Amer-Yahia et al., 2009a], in order to build communities, facilitate search and recommendations. SocialScope is an architecture designed to aggregate data from content and social sites, while Jelly is a language that provides primitives (rating, tagging, users, and items) that can be used to find the relations between users and/or contents. Form SocialScope architecture and Jelly primitives, users can derive topics of interest, community, recommendations, ranking, and explanations.

Exploiting friendship and trust enriches users' profiles enabling to compute a trust value for a given recommendation. In addition, social activities may be taken into account to refine users' profile, improving the quality of recommendation. Notice that tagging activities may be used to capture users profiles. In the remainder of this chapter the term social data refers alternatively to friendship links, tagging activity, and trust.

3.2 P2P CONTENT MANAGEMENT

Recall that RSs have roots in IR systems. IR deals with searching for the contents that match a given query, and then retrieve those contents to the users. RSs take advantage of user preferences, similarities and rates to recommend the best contents. The common feature among these two fields is search for content. In this section, we give an overview of the P2P solutions for content management because they use some interesting techniques that may be useful for P2P recommendation.

P2P systems, such as Gnutella and Kaaza [Liang et al., 2006], support a keyword query capability to search for the contents whose name or description match the keywords. To improve the quality of content retrieval, instead of basic keyword search, IR techniques (e.g., similarities measures, topic and profile extraction techniques, clustering, etc.). have been adapted to be implemented on top of P2P overlays. This implementation provides a way to link peers according to the contents they store and enhances the quality of content retrieval. P2P content management systems are classified according to the way in which their overlays are built as follows.

- **Clustering overlay**. These systems group similar peers with respect to the contents they store in logical clusters.

- **Short link overlay**. In these systems, peers establish direct links with other peers which are similar with respect to interests or social data. These links can either be replaced or added dynamically.

The following sections present existing solutions for these two categories. Section 3.2.1 presents in more detail the clustering overlays. Shortcut links overlays solutions are presented in Section 3.2.2 .

3.2.1   CLUSTERING OVERLAYS

In these systems, content semantics is exploited as clustering criteria. These systems are classified into *peer clustering* and *data clustering*. In peer clustering, peers that have similar contents are grouped together, while in data clustering, contents that have some similarity are placed in selected peers.

Peer Clustering. Peers with similar contents are logically grouped into clusters in order to improve search performance [Bawa et al., 2003, Iamnitchi et al., 2002, Jin et al., 2006, Klampanos and Jose, 2004]. Thus, according to the similarity criteria several clusters are built over an unstructured overlay. A query is then directed to the cluster that is more likely to have answers to the query. Within a cluster, the query is flooded to perform document search. For instance, Garcia-Molina and Crespo [2003] introduce the concept of *semantic overlay* by using peer clustering and a specific content classification hierarchy. Each peer that joins the system, identifies which cluster(s) to join by acquiring the classification hierarchy and classifying its documents against it. Once a peer identifies which cluster(s) it belongs, through flooding, it is able to locate and join them.

The SETS system [Bawa et al., 2003] clusters peers based on their documents' topics. A fixed set C of topic-segments is predetermined, where each topic-segment represents a cluster, and all peers in a cluster store documents related to the topic-segment of that cluster.

Data Clustering. These systems cluster similar contents, with respect to their semantics, in selected peers; for instance, peers that belong to the same locality [Bender et al., 2005, Lv and Cheng, 2004, Sahin et al., 2004, Tang et al., 2003]. Typically, these systems use a structured overlay for document placement. PSearch [Tang et al., 2003] uses a landmark technique to distribute documents in CAN (Content -Addressable Network) DHT [Ratnasamy et al., 2001] (see Chapter 1 for more details). Hence, the documents that are semantically similar also appear physically close to each other in CAN. Accordingly, documents that are relevant to a query are likely to be collocated on a small number of peers in the same locality.

3.2.2   SHORT LINK OVERLAY

In these systems, each peer establishes logical links (shortcut links) with peers that may have contents related to its queries. A query is forwarded first to those links. If a user is not satisfied or the search fails, then the query is routed using flooding. These systems are classified into *interest-based* and *social-based* according to the data that are used to establish the shortcut links. In interest-based, shortcut links are established according to queries log history, or peer interests. In this case, peer interests may be defined either explicitly or implicitly. Social-based systems exploit user social data and behavior, such as tagging activities, friend network, bookmarks, etc. to establish the shortcut links.

Interested-based. These systems [Sripanidkulchai et al., 2003b], [Busnel and Kermarrec, 2007], [Cholvi et al., 2004], [Iamnitchi and Foster, 2005], [Upadrashta et al., 2005] are based on the assumption that if a peer p_i has content that another peer p_j requested or is interested in, then most probably p_i will have other content that may interest p_j. Thus, in these systems each peer p adds links to peers whose interests are similar to p's, interests, or that have successfully answered p's queries. Cholvi et al. [2004] propose a solution that enables each peer to add shortcut links to similar peers in terms of interests, to enhance Gnutella search performance. In their model, each peer is interested in a set of categories of interests. A category of interest is defined as a bag that consists of keywords or topics. Peer categories of interests are either extracted implicitly from peer documents, or stated explicitly by the user. Whenever a peer submits a query, shortcuts are selectively exploited. According to their results, the shortcut links reduces response time as well as the number of exchanged messages.

Similarly, as Sripanidkulchai et al. [2003a] and Upadrashta et al. [2005] propose, each peer p adds shortcut links to the peers that have most recently and successfully answered p's queries. When p searches for contents, it disseminates its query to its shortcuts and, if the search fails, it uses flooding to search within the underlying P2P overlay.

Social-based. These systems consider social data (e.g., friendship links, tagging activities) in constructing the overlay and searching for contents [Chirita et al., 2004, Marti et al., 2004, Upadrashta et al., 2005].

SPROUT [Marti et al., 2004] exploits users' explicit friends on top of the Chord DHT (Distributed Hash Table), in order to avoid misrouting, and increases the number of query results. When a peer p joins the DHT, in addition to its routing table, p adds shortcut links to all its online friends. Once p issues a query q with key k (hash of the content name), it forwards q to the friend f whose peer id is closest to, but not greater than k. Recursively, f forwards q in the same manner until the peer which is responsible for k is found. In case p does not find a friend that satisfies these conditions, then the regular lookup algorithm is used.

Bai et al. [2010] propose a personalized P2P top-k search for collaborative tagging systems, called P4Q, is proposed. In P4Q, each user u maintains locally a profile, noted $profile(u)$, which includes the items that u has tagged along with their tags. In addition, it maintains a personal network, noted $network(u)$, that includes a fixed number n of users with similar interest. $network(u)$

consists of two parts: the first includes the c users that have the highest similarity with u, noted $profileList(u)$, along with their profiles such that $c \ll n$. The second part includes the less similar users along with their profiles stored in a space-efficient data structure called bloom filter, noted $bloomfilter\text{-}List(u)$. Two users are considered similar if they share a common number of tagged items. Notice that Peer Sampling is used to establish $network(u)$ of a user u.

When a user u issues a query (a set of tags), u (or the system on behalf of u) exploits the user profiles of its $profileList(u)$ to process locally the query. If the search fails, or u is not satisfied with the results, u gossips its query as follows. First, u selects from its $bloomfilter\text{-}List(u)$ the users that have tags similar to the query's tags, and adds them to a list, called $remainingList(u)$. Once the $remainingList(u)$ is established, u selects randomly a user v from the $remainingList(u)$ and forwards the query along with the $remainingList(u)$ to v. The remaining list is then recursively exploited to answer the query based on a sophisticated gossip algorithm.

3.3   P2P RECOMMENDATION

Centralized RS solutions may have limited scalability because the time consumed to compute users neighbors and the space required to store the user-item matrix increase exponentially with respect to the number of users and items. Decentralized infrastructures such as P2P systems yield scalability and have been exploited to build distributed RSs.

In P2P recommendation systems, recommendation data (the user-item matrix, users' profiles or social data) are distributed or replicated over the participant users. Therefore, users collaborate to share their contents and generate recommendations. P2P RSs are classified according to the recommendation data that is used to generate recommendations, as follows.

- **Basic P2P prediction**. Recommendations are generated based on users' ratings only.

- **Social P2P prediction**. Users' social data and rates are used in constructing the overlay and generating recommendations.

3.3.1   BASIC P2P PREDICTION

Recall that in centralized RSs, a single provider is responsible for providing recommendations based on a huge user-item matrix. In contrast, in basic P2P prediction systems, each peer keeps a fragment of the user-item matrix. In general, at each peer u, recommendation is done by retrieving and aggregating u neighbors' profiles over the P2P overlay based on similarity measures. This process produces u's fragment of the user-item matrix. Then, u performs locally a traditional Top-k algorithm and generates recommendations with respect to its most similar neighbors contents.

In PocketLens [Miller et al., 2004], recommendation is based on collaborative filtering. The authors explore four P2P solutions including *random discovery* (similar to Gnutella), *transitive traversal*, *distributed hash table*, and *secure blackboard*. In the three solutions, Pearson Correlation Coefficient is used to measure similarity. What differs is the way in which new neighbors are discovered.

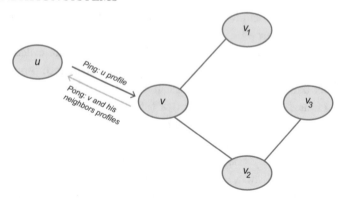

Figure 3.3: Collaborative filtering over an unstructured overlay.

In random discovery, when a user u joins the system, it sends a ping message to each neighbor. Each neighbor v receives a ping message with u's profile (rating on items), and returns a pong message that includes v's profile as well as v's direct overlay neighbors profiles. Once u receives a pong message, it aggregates its similar neighbors from the pong message. In the example of Figure 3.3, u forwards a ping message to its neighbors v. User v returns to u a pong message that includes v's overlay neighbors profiles. Thus, u becomes aware of the existence of new users.

In the transitive traversal, each user u finds new neighbors along with query routing in the following way. u floods its query over an unstructured overlay, and u considers each user v in the response path of the query as a potential new neighbour. Notice that in this approach, each peer only stores profiles of its neighbors (similar peers).

In the DHT solution, a DHT is used to store items and ratings on items. Similar items with their corresponding profile (user, items rate) are stored together in a same peer over the DHT using a specific item identification method (similar items have similar keys). For a given user u, recommendation is done as follows. First u aggregates similar item profiles from the DHT. Then it generates the recommendation using collaborative filtering techniques. Different from random discovery and transitive traversal, the DHT solution avoids profile replication. Simulation results shows that PocketLens recommendation results are close to those obtained by using centralized recommendation.

Han et al. [2004] propose PipeCF to store users' rating over a DHT in order to distribute the user-item matrix. All users that have rated an item with the same rating are grouped in one cluster, called *bucket*. These buckets are spread over the DHT. The item's name and rating are used to generate the key of each bucket (see Figure 3.4). For a given user u, recommendation is done by aggregating buckets of u items.

Finally, Kermarrec et al. [2010] use gossiping and random walk for decentralized RS. Gossip algorithms let each user dynamically retrieve and aggregate its neighbor's profiles. Recommendation

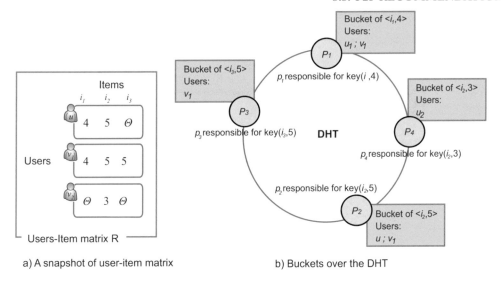

Figure 3.4: Collaborative filtering over a DHT overlay.

is provided based on the neighbors' profiles (items and rates), combined with a specific random walk algorithm. Notice that cosine similarity is used to measure the similarity between users.

3.3.2   SOCIAL P2P PREDICTION SYSTEMS

These systems leverage user's preferences (ratings) with user's social data (friends, trust, etc.) in order to improve recommendation quality and performance in a distributed manner. Exploiting friendship network and trust enables each user to have its own user-item matrix because only trusted friends' rating are aggregated for recommendation. To the best of our knowledge, there are very few social P2P prediction solutions.

Massa and Avesani [2004] propose a trust-aware collaborative filtering that uses user's trust information, in a P2P manner. In this solution, each user u expresses its level of trust, denoted $trust(u, v)$, to every other user v it has interacted with. The $trust(u, v)$ value is between 0 and 1, where 0 means total distrust and 1 means full trust. The trust network is modeled as a directed graph $G = (U, E)$, where U is the set of users in the network, and E is the set of edges between users. There is an edge $e(u, v)$ from user u to user v, if u has expressed its level of trust on user v. The trust level among unknown users u and v is predicted based on a maximum propagation distance d, the minimum distance n between u and v, defined as:

$$trust(u, v) = \frac{d - n + 1}{d}, \tag{3.1}$$

where d is computed based on the number of hops. In the example of Figure 3.5, we assume that the maximum propagation distance d is 4. Then the predicted trust value from u to v is 0.75, and the

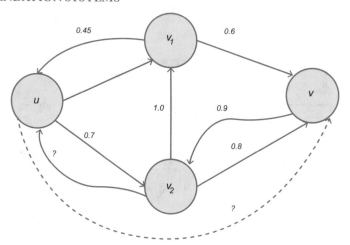

Figure 3.5: Example of trust network.

predicted trust value from v_2 to u is 1. Once u measures the trust level between itself and each user in the network, it selects the most trustful users to be his trusted neighbors, denoted $neighbor_{trust}(u)$. Those neighbors profiles are used to compute the recommendation.

P2Prec is a social-based P2P recommendation solution for large-scale content sharing [Draidi et al., 2011a,b]. The main idea is to recommend high relevant documents related to query topics and contents hold by useful friends (of friends) of the users, by exploiting friendship networks. P2Prec recommendation model relies on a distributed graph, where each node represents a user (peer) labeled with the contents it stores and its topics of interests. The topics each peer is interested in are automatically calculated by analyzing the documents the peer holds. Peers become relevant for a topic if they hold a certain number of highly rated documents on this topic. A peer v becomes useful to a peer u, if u's topics of interest and v's relevant topics are overlapped. To exploit friendship links, we rely on Friend-of-A-Friend (FOAF) descriptions [1]. To disseminate information about relevant peers, gossip algorithms are used that provide scalability, robustness, simplicity, and load balancing.

Each user u exploits its *local-view* to establish friendship. As shown in Figure 3.6, each user manages a *local-view* and each entry of the view corresponds to a specific user information that includes:

$$\langle\, user\text{-}id,\ topics\ of\ interests\ (and\ relevant\ topics),\ friendship\ network\,\rangle\,.$$

For instance, in user v_2's *local-view* in v_4's entry, the expression $(t_2, 1), (t_3, 0)$ means that user v_4's topics of interests are t_2 and t_3. However, the value 1 on the right side of t_2 (noted $(t_2, 1)$)

[1]http://www.foaf-project.org. Accessed on December 2011

means that t_2 is a relevant topic (topics of the highly rated contents) for v_4. In addition, notice that v_4's friends are v_1 and v_2.

At each gossip cycle, u goes through each user entry $v\ddot{i}f^\wedge \in \mathit{local\text{-}view_u}$, and evaluates whether v may be suggested for friendship as follows: user u computes the *similarity* between u and v. The degree of similarity between u and v takes into account the *usefulness* of v and the overlap of their friend network. Notice that user u and v may be similar in terms of topics of interest. However, v may not be useful for u, because the topics of interest of u are not related to v's relevant topics. The usefulness of v with respect to u is computed by counting the overlap between u's topics of interests and v's relevant topics.

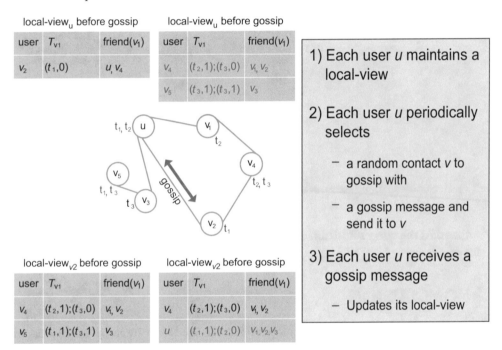

Figure 3.6: Example of gossip exchange.

If u has accepted to establish friendship with v, then it adds v's profile information in its FOAF file. The profile information includes v's relevant topics of interest, a trust value $trust(u, v)$ between u and v, and a link to v's FOAF file that is used during query routing.

Different than content-based filtering, P2Prec provides recommendation once a user submits a keyword query. Once a given peer u submits a query to retrieve documents, the problem is to find u's most useful friends who can provide interesting recommendations. Using the FOAF file at u, the query routing algorithm selects the best peers to recommend documents based on u's most useful friends with respect to the query topics. This algorithm is recursively executed at each selected friend until a specific TTL (Time To Live). These selected peers then propose recommendations to the

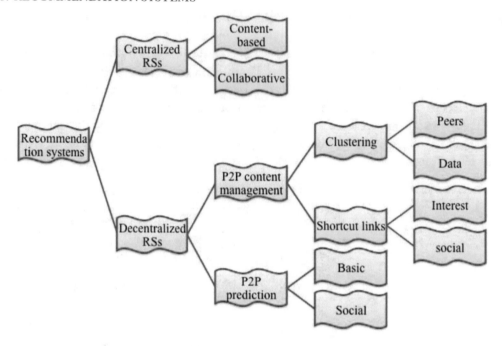

Figure 3.7: Recommendation framework.

query initiator. At the query's initiator, recommendations are selectively chosen based on similarity, rates, and popularity or other ad-hoc recommendation criteria.

3.4 CONCLUSION

In this chapter, we dealt with recommendation for decentralized infrastructures where users wish to keep their contents (documents, items, images, tables, etc.) in their own workspace, which is typically the case for on-line communities. In this context, P2P is appropriate as the underlying infrastructure. Figure 3.7 summarizes centralized and P2P recommendation techniques, and Figure 3.8 presents a general system P2P architecture for P2P content management and P2P recommendation.

Decentralized recommendation infrastructures can be classified between *P2P content management* and *P2P prediction systems*. In P2P content management systems, users submit keywords queries and the system returns a set of contents that are most related to the query. These solutions strive to reduce responses times and network traffic consumed by query routing, not taking into account users' feedbacks and ratings, etc. Therefore, there is no guarantee of the quality of the returned contents.

P2P content management systems use IR techniques, such as clustering, to enhance responses times. Two main approaches are identified: *clustering overlays* and *shortcut links overlays*.

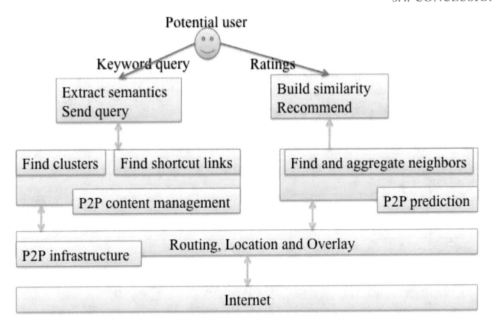

Figure 3.8: P2P recommendation architecture.

In clustering overlays, similar peers with respect to their contents are grouped in one cluster usually on top of an unstructured overlay, or similar contents are placed on the selected peers. Therefore, a query is routed over the P2P overlay to find the adequate cluster to serve the query.

Shortcut links overlays enables each user to establish logical links to users with similar interests, usually on top of an unstructured or dynamic overlay (gossip-based). Shortcut link overlays typically propose specific protocols to search for potential users in order to establish links, exploiting users' interests or social data. We observed that using users' social data such as friends, trust, etc. increases the recommendation quality, and enhances the performance of the system. In unstructured overlays, flooding is used to search for potential shortcuts. In dynamic overlays, gossip protocols are used to search for useful shortcuts links by exploiting users local views. The use of gossip protocols facilitates scalability with acceptable background traffic.

P2P prediction systems proactively return a set of recommendations to users based on their profiles (item and rates). These solutions focus on how to distribute fragments of the user-item matrix over users. We identified two categories of P2P prediction systems: *Basic P2P prediction* and *social-based*. In basic P2P RS, a user searches for its neighbors over the P2P overlay to perform recommendation. The way neighbor profiles are aggregated depends on the underlying P2P overlay. Social-based P2P RSs exploit users' social data such as trust, friends, etc. to provide more personalization to recommendation.

Most of the basic and social P2P prediction systems are built on top of unstructured overlays, and flooding is used to find neighbors. Again, aggregating neighbors' profiles (users' preferences, FOAF files, etc.), using flooding increases network traffic, and this may deteriorate responses times. Structured overlay reduces the network traffic for aggregating neighbors' profiles, but in case of dynamicity introduces some maintenance overhead. Finally, dynamic overlays (gossip-based) are simple to implement and have shown nice properties for scalability.

CHAPTER 4

Top-k Query Processing in P2P Systems

Top-k queries have attracted considerable interest in many different areas such as network and system monitoring [Koudas et al., 2004], information retrieval [Tran et al., 2009], sensor networks [Wu et al., 2006], probabilistic databases [Soliman et al., 2007], multimedia databases [Chaudhuri et al., 2004], spatial data analysis [Hjaltason and Samet, 2003], data stream management systems [Jin et al., 2010], [Das et al., 2007], temporal databases[Li et al., 2010], etc. Given a dataset D and a scoring function f, a top-k query retrieves the k tuples in D with the highest scores according to f. In a large-scale P2P system, top-k queries are very useful [Balke et al., 2005]; they can reduce the network traffic significantly and avoid overwhelming the user with large numbers of uninteresting answers. As an example, assume a community of car dealers who want to take advantage of a P2P system to share some data about the used cars they sell. Assume they agree on a common Car description in relational format. The Cars relation includes attributes such as car-id, price, mileage, mark, model, picture, etc. Suppose a user wants to submit the following query to obtain the 10 top answers ranked by a scoring function over price and mileage:

    SELECT car-id, price, mileage
    FROM Cars
    WHERE (price < 3000) AND (mileage < 60000)
    ORDER BY scoring-function(price, mileage) ASC
    STOP AFTER 10

The user specifies the scoring function according to the criteria of interest. For instance, in the query above, the scoring function could be $(20 \times price + mileage)$.

In this chapter, we present the main algorithms developed for top-k processing in distributed and P2P systems. The rest of the chapter is organized as follows. In Section 4.1, we describe the general model of sorted lists, and then based on this model we discuss two fundamental algorithms which are the base for top-k query processing in many distributed and P2P systems. Afterwards, in Section 4.2, we present some important work for top-k query evaluation in distributed systems. Then, in Section 4.3, we review the main top-k algorithms that have been developed for different P2P overlays, i.e., *unstructured, super-peer, and DHT*.

4.1   GENERAL MODEL FOR TOP-K QUERIES

The problem of answering top-k queries in many centralized, distributed, and P2P systems, especially in super-peer overlays, can be modeled as follows [Fagin et al., 2003]. Suppose we have m lists of n data items such that each data item has a local score in each list and the lists are sorted according to the local scores of their data items. And each data item has an overall score which is computed based on its local scores in all lists using a given scoring function. Then the problem is to find the k data items whose overall scores are the highest. This problem model is simple and general. Let us illustrate with the following examples. Suppose we want to find the top-k tuples in a relational table according to some scoring function over its attributes. To answer this query, it is sufficient to have a sorted (indexed) list of the values of each attribute involved in the scoring function, and return the k tuples whose overall scores in the lists are the highest. As another example, suppose we want to find the top-k documents whose aggregate rank is the highest with regard to some given keywords. To answer this query, the solution is to have for each keyword a sorted list of documents, and return the k documents whose aggregate rank in all lists are the highest.

There has been much work on efficient top-k query processing over sorted lists. A naïve algorithm is to scan all lists from beginning to end, and maintain the local scores of each data item, compute the overall scores, and return the k highest scored data items. However, this algorithm is executed in $O(m \times n)$ and thus is inefficient for large lists of data items.

The best known algorithm for answering top-k queries over sorted lists is the Threshold Algorithm (TA) [Fagin et al., 2001], [Güntzer et al., 2000], [Nepal and Ramakrishna, 1999]. Many distributed and P2P top-k query processing algorithms are based on the TA algorithm that is itself based on Fagin's Algorithm (FA). In this section, we first formally define the sorted lists model, and then we briefly describe FA and TA.

Sorted Lists Model

The sorted lists can be defined as follows. Let D be a set of n data items, and $L_1, L_2, \ldots, L_m$ be m lists such that each list L_i contains n pairs of the form $(d, s_i(d))$ where $d \in D$ and $s_i(d)$ is a non-negative real number that denotes the local score of d in L_i. Any data item $d \in D$ appears once and only once in each list. Each list L_i is sorted in descending order of its local scores, hence called *sorted list*. Let j be the number of data items which are before a data item d in a list L_i, then the *position* of d in L_i is equal to $(j + 1)$.

In a distributed system, sorted lists may be maintained at different nodes. A node that maintains a list is called a *list owner*. In centralized systems, the owner of all lists is only one node.

For each data item d, there is an *overall score* that is computed as $f(s_1(d), s_2(d), \ldots, s_m(d))$ where f is a given *scoring function*. In other words, the overall score is the output of f where the input is the local scores of d in all lists. In many algorithms, the scoring function is assumed to be monotonic. A function f is monotonic if $f(x_1, \ldots, x_m) \leq f(y_1, \ldots, y_m)$ whenever $x_i \leq y_i$ for every i. Many of the popular aggregation functions (such as Min, Max, and Average) are monotonic.

The k data items whose overall scores are the highest among all data items, are called the *top-k data items*.

In many algorithms two data access modes are used for reading the data from sorted lists. The first mode is *sorted access* by which the next data item in the sorted list is accessed. Sorted access begins by accessing the first data item of the list. The second mode of access is *random access* by which a given data item in the list is searched and accessed.

FA

The basic idea of FA (Fagin's Algorithm) [Fagin, 1999] is to scan the lists until at least k data items have been seen in all lists, so there is no need to continue scanning the remainder of the lists [Fagin, 1999]. Given sorted lists $L_1, L_2, \ldots, L_m$, FA works as follows.

1. Do sorted access in parallel to each of the m sorted lists, and maintain each seen data item in a set S. If there are at least k data items in S such that each of them has been seen in each of the m lists, then stop doing sorted access to the lists.

2. For each data item $d \in S$, if d has not been seen in some list L_i, then do random access to L_i in order to read the local score of d in L_i. Compute the overall score of d, and maintain it in a set Y if its score is one of the k highest scores computed so far.

3. Return Y.

Let us illustrate FA with the following example.

Example 4.1   Consider the database (i.e., three sorted lists) shown in Figure 4.1. Assume a top-3 query $Q, k = 3$, and suppose the scoring function computes the sum of the local scores of the data item in all lists. In this example, before position 7, there is no data item that can be seen in all lists, so FA cannot stop before this position. After doing the sorted access at position 7, FA sees d_5 and d_8, which are seen in all lists, but this is not sufficient for stopping sorted access. At position 8, the set of seen data items is $S = \{d_1, d_2, d_3, d_4, d_5, d_6, d_7, d_8, d_9, d_{13}\}$. In S there are 5 items that have been seen in all lists, i.e., $\{d_1, d_3, d_5, d_6, d_8\}$. Thus, at this position, there are at least k data items seen by FA in all lists, so it stops doing sorted access to the lists. Then, for the data items that are seen only in some of the lists (not in all of them), FA does random access and finds their unseen local scores. This is done for $\{d_2, d_4, d_7, d_9, d_{13}\}$. For example, d_2 has not been seen in L_1 so FA needs a random access to L_1 to find the local score of d_2 in this list. Finally, FA computes the overall score of all seen data items, and returns to the user the k highest scored ones.

TA

TA algorithm improves FA by revising the *stopping condition*, i.e., the condition to stop sorted accesses. The stopping condition of TA is based on a threshold that is computed using the last local scores seen under sorted access in each of the lists. The number of sorted accesses done by TA is

Position	List 1 Data item	List 1 Local score	List 2 Data item	List 2 Local score	List 3 Data item	List 3 Local score
1	d_1	30	d_2	28	d_3	30
2	d_4	28	d_6	27	d_5	29
3	d_9	27	d_7	25	d_8	28
4	d_3	26	d_5	24	d_4	25
5	d_7	25	d_9	23	d_2	24
6	d_8	23	d_1	21	d_6	19
7	d_5	17	d_8	20	d_{13}	15
8	d_6	14	d_3	14	d_1	14
9	d_2	11	d_4	13	d_9	12
10	d_{11}	10	d_{14}	12	d_7	11
...	...	...	...	...	...	...

Figure 4.1: Example of three sorted lists.

always less than or equal to that of FA [Fagin et al., 2003]. Given sorted lists $L_1, L_2, \ldots, L_m$, TA works as follows.

1. Do sorted access in parallel to each of the m sorted lists. As a data item d is seen under sorted access in some list, do random access to the other lists to find the local score of d in every list, and compute the overall score of d. Maintain in a set Y the k seen data items whose overall scores are the highest among all data items seen so far.

2. For each list L_i, let s_i be the last local score seen under sorted access in L_i. Define the threshold to be $\delta = f(s_1, s_2, \ldots, s_m)$. If Y involves k data items whose overall scores are greater than or equal to δ, then stop doing sorted access to the lists. Otherwise, go to Step 1.

3. Return Y.

Let us illustrate TA with the following example.

Example 4.2 Consider the three sorted lists shown in Figure 4.1 and the query Q of Example 4.1, with $k = 3$ and a scoring function that computes the sum of the local scores. TA first looks at the data items that are at position 1 in all lists, i.e., d_1, d_2, and d_3. It looks up the local score of these data items in other lists using random access and computes their overall scores. The overall score of each data is computed by applying the scoring function on its local scores. In this example the scoring function is sum. Thus, for example the overall score of d_1 is computed as $f(d_1) = 30 + 21 + 14 = 65$. Notice that the local score of d_1 in L_1 has been seen under sorted access, and its other local scores have been read by random access. The overall scores of d_2 and d_3 are 63 and 70, respectively. The threshold is computed by applying the scoring function on the last scores seen under sorted access. Thus, the threshold is $30 + 28 + 30 = 88$. The overall score of none of the seen data items is as high as the threshold of position 1. Thus, TA does not stop. At this position, we have $Y = \{d_1, d_2, d_3\}$ that is the set of k highest scored data items seen so far. At positions 2 and 3, Y involves $\{d_3, d_4, d_5\}$ and $\{d_3, d_5, d_8\}$, respectively. Before position 6, none of the data items involved in Y has an overall score higher than or equal to the threshold value. At position 6, the threshold value is $23 + 21 + 19 = 63$, which is less than the overall score of the three data items involved in $Y = \{d_3, d_5, d_8\}$. Notice that the overall scores of d_3, d_5 and d_8 are $70, 70$, and 71, respectively. Thus, there are k data items whose overall scores are higher than or equal to the threshold value, so TA stops at position 6.

4.2   TOP-K QUERIES IN DISTRIBUTED SYSTEMS

In a distributed system, the number of messages that a top-k query processing algorithm communicates over the network should be as low as possible. In this section, we present three approaches that have been proposed aiming at optimizing the communication cost of top-k query evaluation in distributed systems. Their base model is that of sorted lists; they assume that the database is partitioned vertically and the partitions are distributed over the nodes of the system.

TPUT

The Three Phase Uniform Threshold (TPUT) [Cao and Wang, 2004] is an efficient algorithm to answer top-k queries in distributed systems. Like TA, TPUT uses a threshold for finding top-k answers. But, its communication cost is usually much lower than that of a direct utilization of TA in distributed systems [Cao and Wang, 2004].

Let us assume that the database is vertically partitioned, and each partition is represented by a sorted list on a node that we call the holder of the list. Then, TPUT executes top-k queries in three rounds as follows.

1. Each list holder sends to the query originator its k top data items, i.e., the k data items whose local scores in the list are the highest. Let f be scoring function, d be a received data item, and $s_i(d)$ be the local score of d in list i, then the partial sum of d is defined as $psum(d) = s'_1(d) + s'_2(d) + \cdots + s'_m(d)$ where $s'_i(d) = s_i(d)$ if d has been sent to the query originator from the holder of list i, otherwise $s_{i}(d) = 0$. The query originator calculates the partial sums for all received data items and identifies the items with the k highest partial sums. The partial sum of the kth data item is called phase-1 bottom and denoted by λ_1.

2. The query originator sends a threshold value $\tau = \lambda_1/m$ to every list holder. Then, each list holder sends to the query originator all its data items whose local scores are not less than τ. The intuition is that if a data item is not reported by any node in this phase, its score must be less than λ_1, so it cannot be one of the top-k data items. Let D be the set of data items received from list holders, the query originator calculates the new partial sums for the data items involved in D, and identifies the items with the k highest partial sums. The partial sum of the kth data item is called phase-2 bottom, and denoted by λ_2. Let the upper bound score of

a data item d be defined as $uscore(d) = u_1(d) + u_2(d) + \cdots + u_m(d)$ where $u_i(d) = s_i(d)$ if d has been received from the holder of list i, otherwise $u_i(d) = \tau$. For each data item $d \in D$, if the upper bound score of d is less than λ_2, it is removed from D. The data items that remain in D are called the top-k candidate data items.

3. The query originator sends the set of top-k candidate data items to the list holders, and they return back the scores of these items. Then, the query originator calculates the overall scores, extracts the k data items with highest scores, and returns the answer to the user.

Let us illustrate TPUT by the following example.

Example 4.3   Consider the three nodes shown in Figure 4.2. Assume L_1 and L_2 are the lists maintained by nodes N_1 and N_2, respectively. Assume node N_3 issues a query Q with $k = 2$, and suppose the scoring function computes the sum of the local scores of each data item. Let us apply TPUT on this example. In the first step of TPUT, the nodes N_1 and N_2 send their k first data items to N_3 who computes the partial sums for the received data as follows. $p_{sum}(t_3) = 70$, $p_{sum}(t_2) = 36$, and $p_{sum}(t_1) = 30$. The kth partial sum is 36, thus the phase-1 bottom λ_1 is equal to 36. Therefore, we have $\tau = \lambda_1/m = 36/2 = 18$. Notice that m is the number of lists. In Phase 2, the query originator sends τ to the list holders, and they return all data items whose local scores are higher than τ. The union of data items received from N_1 and N_2 is $D = \{t_1, t_2, t_3, t_6\}$. Now, the partial sums for the received data are as follows: $p_{sum}(t_3) = 70$, $p_{sum}(t_1) = 52$, $p_{sum}(t_6) = 51$, and $p_{sum}(t_2) = 36$. The partial sum of the kth data item is $\lambda_2 = 52$. The upper bound scores of the data items involved in the set D are as follows: $u_{score}(t_3) = 70$, $u_{score}(t_1) = 52$, $u_{score}(t_6) = 51$, and $u_{score}(t_2) = 54$. Since the upper bound score of t_6 is lower than λ_2, the query originator removes it form D, and the list of candidate data items becomes $D = \{t_1, t_2, t_3\}$. Among the data items in D, only t_2 has an unknown score. Thus, in Phase 3, t_2 is sent to N_1 in order to return the missing score. Then, the query originator chooses the top-2 results among the candidate data items.

Although TPUT usually works better than TA, there are specific cases where TPUT is not efficient [Cao and Wang, 2004]. For example, if one of the lists has n data items with the same value that is greater than the threshold τ, then all data items must be retrieved by the query originator, while a more adaptive algorithm might avoid retrieving all n data items.

Threshold Join Algorithm

Threshold Join Algorithm (TJA) [Zeinalipour-Yazti et al., 2005] has been proposed for top-k query processing in the context of sensor networks. There are some similarities between TJA and TPUT. For example, both of them proceed in three phases. But, the thresholds that they use for reducing the communication cost are not the same. In addition, with TJA the query messages are forwarded from the query originator to the list holders (i.e., those that maintain the sorted lists) via intermediate nodes in a graph, not directly.

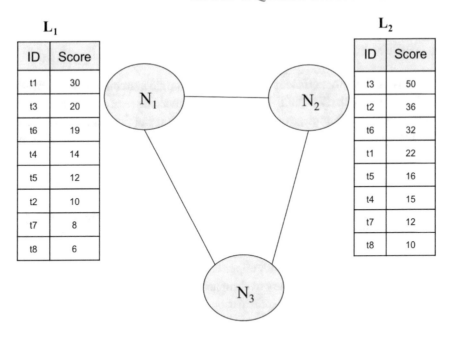

Figure 4.2: Example of three nodes in a distributed system. The score lists of nodes N_1 and N_2 are shown aside them.

Let us shortly describe TJA that works in the following phases: Lower Bounding (LB), Hierarchal Join (HJ), and Clean-Up (CU):

- In the LB phase, the query originator forwards the query to the list holders, and each list holder sends to the query originator (via the intermediate nodes) the set of k data items with highest local scores.

- In the second phase, the query originator creates a set L_{total} that is the union of all received data items, and forwards it to list holders. Each node looks at its local data and finds the position, say p, of the lowest scored data item in L_{total}. It returns to its parent the local data items whose position is higher than p. The parent of a node is the one from which it receives the query. The intermediate nodes combine the results received from their children, and compute an upper bound for the data items that are *incomplete*, i.e., some of their local score are unknown. The upper bound is computed in a similar way as that of TPUT, by substituting the unknown scores by the lower bounds.

- Let us denote as *exact* the data items whose scores are known entirely. In the third phase, the query originator discards the k data items whose upper bound score is lower than the kth highest scored *exact* data item. Then it retrieves the unknown local scores of the remaining incomplete data items by requesting from the list holders. After receiving the requested scores, the query originator computes the overall score of all data items, and returns to the user the k data items with the highest overall scores.

Although TJA is usually more efficient than TA in distributed systems, there are cases where it can be very inefficient, particularly when there is a high variance between the positions of data items in different sorted lists. For example, assume two lists such that the first data of each list is at the end of the other list. In this case, the second phase of TJA will move all data items of each node to the query originator.

KLEE

KLEE [Michel et al., 2005] is an approximate TA-style algorithm that aims at gaining much reduction in communication cost with limited reduction in result quality. In KLEE, the m sorted lists are distributed over m nodes, and each node divides its list into c cells and maintains statistical information about the cells, such as lower bound, upper bound, average, and frequency of local scores that fall in the cell. KLEE uses Bloom filters to compactly represent, for each cell, the set of data items whose local scores fall in the cell. This information on cells along with the Bloom filters contribute to the reduction of the number of local scores that should be communicated over the network, thus reducing communication cost. However, the results returned by KLEE are approximate, particularly because of the utilization of Bloom filters that may return false positives about the presence of data items in the cells.

4.3   TOP-K QUERIES IN P2P SYSTEMS

In this section, we review the main approaches developed for top-k query processing in different P2P overlays: unstructured, super-peer, and DHT.

4.3.1   TOP-K QUERIES IN UNSTRUCTURED OVERLAYS

A major problem of unstructured overlays is their heavy network traffic [Ripeanu et al., 2002b]. A main portion of this traffic is caused by the large amount of query answers, a lot of which may not be of interest to users. One obvious solution to this problem is to send the query only to the peers that are close to the query originator in the overlay. However, this significantly reduces the quality of results, in the sense that the user cannot get potentially *"good"* answers.

Another solution is the usage of top-k queries. In this section, we present the main approaches developed for top-k query processing in unstructured P2P overlays.

PlanetP

PlanetP [Cuenca-Acuna et al., 2003] is an unstructured P2P overlay that supports top-k queries. In PlanetP, a content-addressable publish/subscribe service replicates global documents across P2P communities. The peers publish their data to PlanetP, and a term-to-peer index is computed based on the published data. The index is replicated to all peers using a gossiping technique.

The peers are ranked based on their importance for each term. To rank peers, PlanetP uses a measure called inverse peer frequency (IPF). Let N be the total number of peers and N_t be the number of peers that maintain at least one document containing a term t, then IPF_t (called IPF of t) is computed as $log\ (1 + N/N_t)$. The idea behind IPF is that the more a term is present in peers, the less it is useful for distinguishing the peers. After computing the IPF of each term, the rank of peers for a query Q, denoted as $R_p(Q)$, is computed as follows:

$$R_p(Q) = \sum_{t \in Q | (t,p) \in I} (IPF_t)\,,$$

where I is the term-to-peer index. Intuitively, $R_p(Q)$ is equal to the sum of IPF of all query terms that are present at p.

The top-k query processing algorithm works as follows. Given a query Q, the query originator computes the ranking of peers with respect to Q, contacts them one by one from top of ranking and asks them to return the set of their k top-scored documents. It maintains in a set Y the k highest scored documents received so far. If the documents returned by a peer p does not change the content of Y, then query originator stops contacting the peers, and returns Y to the user. The idea is that if the score of the documents returned by p is lower than all documents in Y, then the other peers cannot change Y, because their rank is lower than p.

In order to reduce the size of its index, PlanetP uses Bloom filters such that each peer summarizes its documents' terms by inserting them in the filter. However, this approach reduces the accuracy of the top-k algorithm due to the possibility of false positives in Bloom filters. The top-k approach of PlanetP can work well in moderate-scale systems. However, in a large P2P system, keeping up-to-date the replicated index is not easy, and this may hurt the performance of the system.

Fully Distributed

The Fully Distributed Algorithm (FD) [Akbarinia et al., 2006] has been developed for applications in which the data are horizontally partitioned over the peers, i.e., each peer maintains some tuples or documents about a topic. Horizontal partitioning is in contrast to vertical partitioning in which each peer maintains the values of one or some attributes of a relation.

FD uses a tree-based structure for processing top-k queries. It proceeds in four phases (see Figure 4.3): query forward, local query execution, merge-and-backward, and data retrieval.

Query Forward. In this phase, the query originator, say p_{int}, initializes the query message by including in it the query Q, its identifier (QID), and a TTL (Time-To-Live) that denotes the number of hops that the query should be forwarded. Then, p_{int} sends the query message to its reachable neighbors. Each peer p that receives the message performs the following steps: (1) Check QID: if Q has been already received, then p discards the message else it saves the address of the sender as its *parent*; (2) Decrement TTL by one: if TTL is greater than zero, p makes a new message

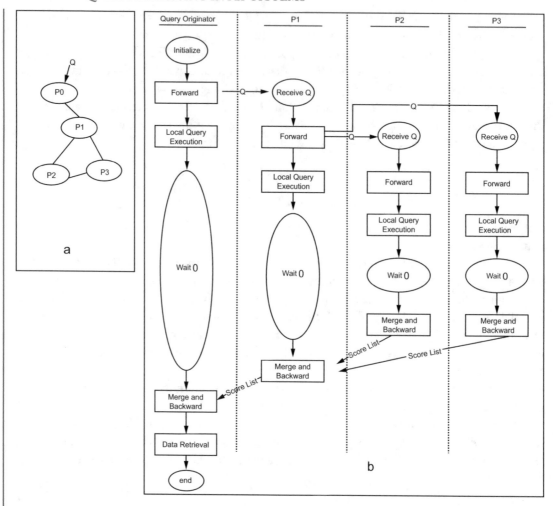

Figure 4.3: (a) A sample P2P overlay; (b) a diagram showing the execution of the FD algorithm by the four peers of the overlay.

including Q, QID, new TTL and the query originator's address, and then it sends the message to all neighbors (except parent).

Local Query Execution. After sending Q to its neighbors, each peer p retrieves the local data items that match the query predicate, scores them using a scoring function, selects the k top data items, and saves them as well as their scores locally. Then, p waits to receive its neighbors' answers before starting the next phase. Since some of the neighbors may leave the P2P system and never send a score-list to p, FD sets a limit for the wait time that is computed mainly based on TTL. The lower is TTL of the query message at a peer, the lower is its wait time.

Merge-and-Backward. After its wait time has expired, each peer p merges its k local top scores with those received from its neighbors and sends the k best scores to its parent (the peer from which it received Q) in the form of a score-list. A *score-list* is simply a list of k pairs (a, s), such that s is a score and a is the address of the peer owning the data item with score s. In order to minimize network traffic, FD does not transfer the top data items (which could be large), only their scores and addresses. If the parent of a peer is no longer available, the score-list is sent directly to the query originator.

Data Retrieval. When the query originator has produced its merged score-list (called the final score-list), it directly contacts the peers whose address appears in the score-list.

HPJT

The Hierarchical P2P Join Top-k (HPJT) algorithm [Guan et al., 2009] can be considered as an adaptation of the TPUT algorithm for unstructured overlays. It assumes a vertical data partitioning. Query processing proceeds as follows. The query originator forwards the query to the peers whose hop distance from it is not higher than a TTL. Let *parent* of a peer p be the first peer from which p receives the query. Each peer p that receives the query sends to its parent the k data items whose local scores in the list are the highest. The received data items from children are bubbled up until reaching the query originator. The query originator computes a partial score for each received data item, and computes a threshold that is equal to $tempKscore/n$ where $tempKscore$ is the sum of partial scores, and n the number of peers that have answered the query. The threshold is forwarded to the peers, and the peers are asked to bubble up all data whose local scores are higher than the threshold. The query originator computes again the partial score of the received data items. It also computes an upper bound score for the data items by substituting the unknown local scores with the maximum possible score. Then, it discards the data items whose upper bound score is lower than the kth partial score. Let us call the remaining data items as *candidate items*. The candidate items are completed by requesting the unknown scores from the peers that maintain the local scores. Then among the candidate items, the query originator chooses the k highest score items as top-k results.

ASAP

Most of the Top-k query processing solutions in unstructured P2P overlays try to reduce the response time while avoiding high network traffic. By response time we mean the time that the query originator is sure that it has found the exact top-k results. In very large P2P systems, even with efficient algorithms, the response time may be high, thus the user may have to wait much. The objective of ASAP framework [Dedzoe et al., 2010] is to return to the user high quality answers as soon as possible (i.e., before returning the final results), in order to reduce the user's wait for relatively good results. For this, in addition to response time, ASAP takes into account two new metrics in processing top-k queries: *stabilization time* and *cumulative quality gap*.

Assume that the query originator receives the candidate top answers from the other peers over a time T, then stabilization time and cumulative quality gap can be defined as follows (see Figure 4.4).

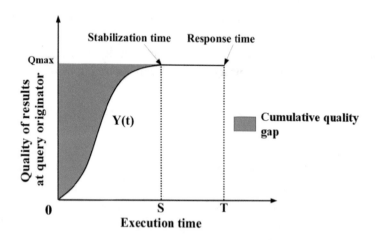

Figure 4.4: Stabilization time and cumulative quality gap wrt response time.

Stabilization time. This is the time at which the query originator has received all final top-k results, without being sure that they are final top-k results. Notice that the response time may be much higher than the stabilization time, because some of the queried peers that do not have good results may return their answers very late.

Cumulative quality gap (Cqg). This is the cumulative gap between the maximum quality (i.e., that of final answers) and the quality of answers at the query originator over time from the beginning to stabilization time. Formally, Cqg can be defined as follows. Let Q be a query, and $Y(t)$ the quality of the answers at time t at the query originator. The quality of answers can be computed for example as the percentage of the final top-k results in the intermediate results received up to time t by the query originator. Let S be the stabilization time of Q, then Cqg is defined as: $Cqg = \int_0^S (1 - Y(t)) dt$.

The objective of ASAP is to develop algorithms that focus on minimizing stabilization time and/or cumulative quality gap while avoiding high communication cost.

Since the objective of ASAP is different from most of other works, its query execution approach is different as well. The main difference between query execution in ASAP and other algorithms such as FD is in its bubbling up phase, when the intermediate peers combine the answers received from their children and send to their parent. In ASPA, intermediate peers do not wait until receiving the answers from all their children, but they send them gradually. A peer's decision to send intermediate results to its parent is based on the improvement impact brought by its current top-k intermediate answers over the answers sent so far. The improvement is computed in two ways: score-based and rank-based.

In the score-based improvement, each peer computes the score gain of its current top-k answer compared to the answers sent so far. In the rank-based improvement, each peer takes into account the loss of rank of the previously sent answers. For example, if the current set of answers is the same as the one sent previously, then the rank-based improvement is zero. For more details about the computation of score-based and rank-based improvements, the reader is referred to [Dedzoe et al., 2010]. The experimental results in [Dedzoe et al., 2010] show that ASAP significantly outperforms baseline algorithms in terms of stabilization time and cumulative quality gap.

4.3.2   TOP-K QUERIES IN SUPER-PEER OVERLAYS

Super-peer overlays typically rely on powerful and highly available peers, called super-peers, to index the data shared by peers connected to the system. In these networks, the queries of each peer are usually sent to its responsible super-peer. The super-peer can then find the relevant peers either directly through its index or indirectly using its neighbor super-peers.

In this section, we present two approaches for top-k query processing in super-peer overlays.

Edutella

Edutella [Balke et al., 2005] is a super-peer overlay in which a small percentage of nodes are super-peers and are assumed to be highly available with very good computing capacity. It assumes horizontal data partitioning.

In Edutella, top-k query processing is done as follows. Given a query Q, the query originator sends Q to its super-peer who forwards it to other super-peers. The super-peers send Q to the relevant peers connected to them. Each peer that has some data items relevant to Q scores them and sends only its maximum scored data item to its super-peer. Each super-peer chooses the maximum scored item from all received data items. For determining the second best item, it only asks the peer that has returned the first top item, to return its second top scored item. Then, the super-peer selects the second top item from the previously received items and the newly received item. Then, it asks the peer that has returned the second top item, to return its next data item. This continues until all k top items will be retrieved. Finally, the super-peers send their top items to the super-peer of the query originator, to extract the k top items, and to send them to the query originator.

Skyline-based

SPEERTO [Vlachou et al., 2008] is a framework that supports top-k queries in super-peer overlays, based on the ideas of Skyline query processing. The data items are assumed to be horizontally partitioned, and the scoring function is monotonic. The maximum number of query results is limited to a predefined number K. Like any other super-peer system, in SPEERTO the super-peers maintain some information about the peers that are associated to them. For processing top-k queries, each super-peer needs to keep the aggregated K-skyband set of its associated peers.

Lest us now present the concept of K-skyband that is used in Skyline query processing. In Skyline queries, given d dimensions (i.e., attributes), the results of the query are the data that are not dominated by any other data. A data d_1 is dominated by another data d_2, if the value of d_2 in each dimension is at least that of d_1, and there is at least one dimension in which the value of d_2 is higher than d_1. A *K-skyband* query returns the data items that are not dominated by more than $K - 1$ other items. An ordinary skyline query is a 1-skyband query.

In SPEERTO, each peer sends to its super-peer the set of its K-skyband, and the super-peers maintain an aggregate K-skyband set of all received sets. The top-k queries (when $k \leq K$) can be answered by the super-peers using the K-skyband set of its data. The core idea is that if a data is dominated by K other data items, i.e., it is not in K-skyband, then it can not appear in the results of a top-K query (notice that the scoring function is monotonic).

The skyline-based approach of SPEERTO can work when the number of dimensions is very small. For high dimensions, the results of a K-skyband query is almost equal to the set of all data items, thus the super-peers have to maintain almost all data items of their associated peers.

4.3.3   TOP-K QUERIES IN DHTS

DHTs offer efficient and scalable support for exact match queries. However, it is quite challenging to support top-k queries on top of DHTs [Blanco et al., 2006]. A simple solution is to retrieve all tuples of the relations involved in the query, and evaluate the top-k query in a centralize way. However, this solution cannot scale up to a large number of tuples. Another solution is to store all tuples of each relation by using the same key, so that all tuples will be stored at the same peer. Then, top-k query processing can be performed at that central peer using well-known centralized algorithms. However, the central peer becomes a bottleneck and single point of failure.

It is possible to design a TA-style algorithm for DHTs. In this section, we describe one such algorithm called DHTop [Akbarinia et al., 2007].

DHTop

Any solution for top-k queries in DHTs depends on the way the data are stored in the peers. We first describe the data storage mechanism of DHTop, and then present the approach for processing top-k queries.

Data Storage

DHTop uses a data storage mechanism that stores the data in the DHT with two complementary methods: tuple storage and attribute-value storage. With the tuple storage method, each tuple of a relation is entirely stored in the DHT using the tuple identifier as the storage key. This enables looking up a tuple by its identifier. Let R be a relation name and A be the set of its attributes. Let T be the set of tuples of R and $id(t)$ be a function that denotes the identifier of a tuple $t \in T$. Let h be a hash function that hashes its inputs into a DHT key, i.e., a number that can be mapped by the DHT onto a peer. For storing the relation R, each tuple $t \in T$ is entirely stored in the DHT where the storage key is $h(R, id(t))$, that is the hash of the relation name and the tuple identifier. Hereafter, the key by which a tuple is stored in the DHT is called tuple storage key.

Attribute-value storage stores in the DHT the attributes that may appear in the query predicates or in the query scoring function. Thus, like database secondary indices, it allows checking for the existence of tuples using attribute values. The attribute-value storage method has two important properties: (1) after retrieving an attribute value from the DHT, peers can retrieve easily the corresponding tuple of the attribute value; (2) attribute values that are relatively "close" are stored at the same peer. To satisfy the first property, the key used for storing the entire tuple is stored along with the attribute value.

The second property is satisfied by using the concept of domain partitioning as follows. Consider an attribute a and let D_a be its domain of values. Assume there is a total order $<$ on D_a. D_a is partitioned into n non-empty sub-domains $d_1, d_2, \ldots, d_n$ such that their union is equal to D_a, the intersection of any two different sub-domains is empty, and for each $v_1 \in d_i$ and $v_2 \in d_j$, if $i < j$ then we have $v_1 < v_2$. Given a value v, the sub-domain to which v belongs is denoted by $sd(a, v)$. The number of sub-domains of an attribute and the lower bound of each sub-domain are known to all peers of the DHT. Therefore, given an attribute a and a value v, any peer can locally compute $sd(a, v)$.

The key that is used for storing an attribute value in the DHT is constructed as follows. Let R be a relation, a be an attribute of R, and v be the value of a in a tuple t, then the key for storing v in the DHT is $h(R, a, sd(a, v))$, i.e., the hash of the relation name, attribute name and the sub-domain to which v belongs. Therefore, the attribute values that belong to the same sub-domain are stored with the same key, and are maintained at the same peer.

Algorithm

The DHTop algorithm is based on the TA algorithm. It works as follows. Let Q be a given top-k query, f its scoring function, and p_{int} the query originator. Let scoring attributes be the attributes that are used in f. DHTop starts at p_{int} and proceeds as follows. For each scoring attribute α, the query originator creates a list L_α and adds all sub-domains of α to it. Then it removes from L_α the sub-domains that do not satisfy Q's condition, and sorts L_α in descending order of its sub-domains. Then for each scoring attribute α and in parallel, p_{int} sends Q to the peer p that is responsible for maintaining the values of α whose sub-domain is $L_\alpha[1]$. The peer p returns to p_{int} the values of α that satisfy Q's condition, one by one in descending order, along with their corresponding tuple storage key. For each received attribute value, p_{int} retrieves the corresponding tuple of v and computes its score. If it is one of the k highest scores, then p_{int} maintains it in a list Y. The stop condition of DHTop is that there are k tuples in Y whose scores are higher than a threshold. If the stop condition holds, then the set Y is returned to the user. If by using the values returned by p the stop condition does not hold, then p_{int} sends Q to the peer that maintains the sub-domain $L_\alpha[2]$. This procedure continues until having k tuples in Y whose scores are higher than the threshold.

The threshold of DHTop is inspired by the TA algorithm and is computed as follows. Let α_1, $\alpha_2, \ldots, \alpha_m$ be the scoring attributes. Let $v_1, v_2, \ldots, v_m$ be the last values received, respectively, for attributes $\alpha_1, \alpha_2, \ldots, \alpha_m$. Then, the DHTop's threshold is defined as $\delta = f(v_1, v_2, \ldots, v_m)$.

In order to reduce the number of messages, an optimized version of DHTop retrieves the attribute values from the peers that are responsible sub-domains in a batch way, i.e., n values per message where n is a predefined value.

Let us illustrate the DHTop algorithm using the following example.

Example 4.4   Consider the top-k query Q below, and assume that the attributes *weight* and *height* are stored in the DHT using the attribute-value storage and by partitioning their domains. For example, assume that the maximum value of attribute weight is 150 (in Kg), and its domain has been partitioned into five sub-domains as follows: $d_1 = [0..40]$, $d_2 = (40..60]$, $d_3 = (60..80]$, $d_4 = (80..110]$, $d_5 = (110..150]$. DHTop creates a list of sub-domains for each scoring attribute, and then removes the sub-domains that cannot satisfy the query. For example, the list of sub-domains for attribute *weight* is initially $L_{weight} = (d_5, d_4, d_3, d_2, d_1)$. Then the sub-domains d_1, d_2, and d_5 are removed from the list, since the query states that *weight* should be between 50 and 100. Thus, we have $L_{weight} = (d_4, d_3, d_2)$. The query originator p_{int} contacts the peer that is responsible of the first sub-domain of each list (for example the responsible of d_4 for attribute *weight*) and asks to return the stored attribute values. Then, p_{int} retrieves the whole tuples, and computes their overall score. If there are k tuples with overall higher than the threshold, then the algorithm stops. Otherwise, p_{int} contacts the peer that is responsible for the second sub-domain, and so on.

> Q: **SELECT** *
> **FROM** *Patient*
> **WHERE** $(50 \leq weight \leq 110)$
> **ORDER BY** scoring-function(*weight, height*) DESC
> **STOP AFTER** 10

4.4   CONCLUSION

In this chapter, we described the main approaches for top-k query processing in distributed and P2P systems. They particularly focus on reducing the number of communicated messages, while taking into account the special features such as the architecture of P2P overlays, and the volatility of peers.

The proposed solutions assume either horizontal or vertical data partitioning. Those that are designed for vertically partitioned data (e.g., TPUT, TJA, KLEE, HPJT, DHTop) usually use algorithms that are close to that of the TA algorithm, but adapted to the requirements of the distributed or P2P systems. They try to develop an efficient threshold-based stop condition in order to stop the data accesses as soon as possible, while trying to minimize the number of messages used for accessing the needed data.

The solutions that assume horizontal data partitioning (e.g., FD, ASAP, Edutella, SPEERTO) generally develop a hierarchical organization for processing top-k queries. For example, FD and ASAP use a tree structure, which is formed when the query is forwarded to the peers. In Edutella and SPEERTO, the organization of super-peers is used for efficient query routing and result ranking. The proposed solutions usually try to not transfer the data for top-k query processing, but only the scores of the data items. The scores that have no chance to be one of the final k scores are filtered in the hierarchical structure.

Bibliography

K. Aberer. *Peer-to-Peer Data Management*. Morgan & Claypool, 2010. DOI: 10.2200/S00338ED1V01Y201104DTM015 Cited on page(s) xii, 41

K. Aberer, P. Cudré-Mauroux, A. Datta, Z. Despotovic, M. Hauswirth, M. Punceva, and R. Schmidt. P-grid: a self-organizing structured p2p system. *ACM SIGMOD Rec.*, 32(3):29–33, 2003. DOI: 10.1145/945721.945729 Cited on page(s) 2

R. Akbarinia, E. Pacitti, and P. Valduriez. Reducing network traffic in unstructured p2p systems using top-k queries. *Distrib. Parall. Databases*, 19(2-3):67–86, 2006. DOI: 10.1007/s10619-006-8313-5 Cited on page(s) 65

R. Akbarinia, E. Pacitti, and P. Valduriez. Processing top-k queries in distributed hash tables. In *Proc. 13th Int. Euro-Par Conf.*, pages 489–502, 2007. DOI: 10.1007/978-3-540-74466-5_53 Cited on page(s) 2, 70

S. Amer-Yahia and Cong Yu. Leveraging communities in social content sites. In *Advances in Database Technology, Proc. 12th Int. Conf. on Extending Database Technology*, page 1, 2009. DOI: 10.1145/1698790.1698792 Cited on page(s) 46

S. Amer-Yahia, M. Benedikt, Laks V. S. Lakshmanan, and J. Stoyanovich. Efficient network aware search in collaborative tagging sites. *Proc. 34th Int. Conf. on Very Large Data Bases*, 1(1):710–721, 2008. Cited on page(s) 44

S. Amer-Yahia, J. Huang, and C. Yu. Jelly: A language for building community-centric information exploration applications. In *Proc. 25th Int. Conf. on Data Engineering*, pages 1588–1594, 2009a. DOI: 10.1109/ICDE.2009.178 Cited on page(s) 46

S. Amer-Yahia, L.V. S. Lakshmanan, and C. Yu. Socialscope: Enabling information discovery on social content sites. In *Proc. 4th Biennial Conf. on Innovative Data Systems Research*, 2009b. Cited on page(s) 46

D. P. Anderson, J. Cobb, E.Korpela, M. Lebofsky, and D. Werthimer. Seti@. *Commun. ACM*, 45 (11):56–61, 2002. DOI: 10.1145/581571.581573 Cited on page(s) 1

S. Androutsellis-Theotokis and D. Spinellis. A survey of peer-to-peer content distribution technologies. *ACM Comput. Surv.*, 36(4):335–371, 2004a. DOI: 10.1145/1041680.1041681 Cited on page(s) 3

S. Androutsellis-Theotokis and D. Spinellis. A survey of peer-to-peer content distribution technologies. *ACM Comput. Surv.*, 36(4):335–371, 2004b. DOI: 10.1145/1041680.1041681 Cited on page(s) 17, 29

X. Bai, M. Bertier, R. Guerraoui, AM. Kermarrec, and V Leroy. Gossiping personalized queries. In *Proc. 13th Int. Conf. on Extending Database Technology*, pages 87–98, 2010. DOI: 10.1145/1739041.1739055 Cited on page(s) 48

M. Balabanovic and Y. Shoham. Content-based, collaborative recommendation. *Commun. ACM*, 40(3):66–72, 1997. DOI: 10.1145/245108.245124 Cited on page(s) 45

W.-T. Balke, W. Nejdl, W. Siberski, and U. Thaden. Progressive distributed top k retrieval in peer-to-peer networks. In *Proc. 21st Int. Conf. on Data Engineering*, pages 174–185, 2005. DOI: 10.1109/ICDE.2005.115 Cited on page(s) 57, 69

M. Bawa, G. Singh Manku, and P. Raghavan. Sets: search enhanced by topic segmentation. In *Proc. 20th Annual Int. ACM SIGIR Conf. on Research and Development in Information Retrieval*, pages 306–313, 2003. DOI: 10.1145/860435.860491 Cited on page(s) 47

M. Bender, S. Michel, P. Triantafillou, G. Weikum, and C. Zimmer. Minerva: Collaborative p2p search. In *Proc. 31st Int. Conf. on Very Large Data Bases*, pages 1263–1266, 2005. Cited on page(s) 47

A. Bhargava, K. Kothapalli, C. Riley, C. Scheideler, and M. Thober. Pagoda: a dynamic overlay network for routing, data management, and multicasting. In *Proc. 16th Annual ACM Symp. on Parallelism in Algorithms and Architectures*, pages 170–179, 2004. DOI: 10.1145/1007912.1007938 Cited on page(s) 1

K. Birman. The promise, and limitations, of gossip protocols. *Operating Systems Rev.*, 41(5):8–13, 2007. DOI: 10.1145/1317379.1317382 Cited on page(s) 16, 17

R. Blanco, N. Ahmed, D. Hadaller, L.G.A. Sung, H. Li, and M.A. Soliman. A survey of data management in peer-to-peer systems. Technical Report CS-2006-18, University of Waterloo, 2006. Cited on page(s) 70

D. M. Blei, A. Y. Ng, and M. I. Jordan. Latent dirichlet allocation. *Journal of Machine Learning Research*, 3:993–1022, 2003. Cited on page(s) 45

B.H. Bloom. Space/time trade-offs in hash coding with allowable errors. *Commun. ACM*, 13(7):422–426, 1970. DOI: 10.1145/362686.362692 Cited on page(s) 8

J. S. Breese, D. Heckerman, and C. Myers Kadie. Empirical analysis of predictive algorithms for collaborative filtering. In *Proc. 14th Conf. on Uncertainty in Artificial Intelligence*, pages 43–52, 1998. DOI: 10.1111/j.1553-2712.2011.01172.x Cited on page(s) 42

Y. Busnel and AM Kermarrec. Proxsem: Interest-based proximity measure to improve search efficiency in p2p systems. In *Proc. 4th European Conf. Universal Multiservice Networks*, pages 62–74, 2007. DOI: 10.1109/ECUMN.2007.44 Cited on page(s) 48

R. Buyya, M. Pathan, and A. Vakali. *Content Delivery Networks*. Springer, 2008. DOI: 10.1007/978-3-540-77887-5 Cited on page(s) 25, 28, 29

Hailong Cai and Jun Wang. Foreseer: A novel, locality-aware P2P system architecture for keyword searches. In *Proc. ACM/IFIP/USENIX 5th Int. Middleware Conf.*, pages 38–58, 2004. Cited on page(s) 21

J. F. Canny. Collaborative filtering with privacy via factor analysis. In *Proc. 25th Annual Int. ACM SIGIR Conf. on Research and Development in Information Retrieval*, pages 238–245, 2002. DOI: 10.1145/564376.564419 Cited on page(s) 44

P. Cao and Z. Wang. Efficient top-k query calculation in distributed networks. In *Proc. ACM SIGACT-SIGOPS 23rd Symp. on the Principles of Distributed Computing*, pages 206–215, 2004. DOI: 10.1145/1011767.1011798 Cited on page(s) 61, 62

M. Castro, M. Costa, and A. I. T. Rowstron. Should we build Gnutella on a structured overlay? *Comp. Comm. Rev.*, 34(1):131–136, 2004. DOI: 10.1145/972374.972397 Cited on page(s) 21

S. Chaudhuri, L. Gravano, and A. Marian. Optimizing top-k selection queries over multimedia repositories. *IEEE Trans. Knowl. and Data Eng.*, 16(8):992–1009, 2004. DOI: 10.1109/TKDE.2004.30 Cited on page(s) 57

R. Cheng and J. Vassileva. User motivation and persuasion strategy for peer-to-peer communities. In *Proc. 40th Annual Hawaii Int. Conf. on System Sciences*, 2005. DOI: 10.1109/HICSS.2005.653 Cited on page(s) 41

PA. Chirita, D.Olmedilla, and W. Nejdl. Pros: A personalized ranking platform for web search. In *Proc. 3rd Int. Conf. Adaptive Hypermedia and Adaptive Web-Based Systems*, pages 34–43, 2004. DOI: 10.1007/978-3-540-27780-4_7 Cited on page(s) 48

V. Cholvi, P. Felber, and E. Biersack. Efficient search in unstructured peer-to-peer networks. *European Transactions on Telecommunications*, 15(6):535–548, 2004. DOI: 10.1002/ett.1017 Cited on page(s) 48

I. Clarke, S. G. Miller, T. W. Hong, O. Sandberg, and B. Wiley. Protecting free expression online with Freenet. *IEEE Internet Comput.*, 6(1):40–49, 2002. DOI: 10.1109/4236.978368 Cited on page(s) 2

E. Cohen and S. Shenker. Replication strategies in unstructured P2P networks. In *Proc. Conf. on Applications, Technologies, Architectures, and Protocols for Computer Communication*, pages 177–190, 2002. DOI: 10.1145/964725.633043 Cited on page(s) 17

A. Crespo and H. Garcia-Molina. Routing indices for peer-to-peer systems. In *Proc. 22nd Int. Conf. on Distributed Computing Systems*, pages 23–33, 2002. DOI: 10.1109/ICDCS.2002.1022239 Cited on page(s) 7

F. M. Cuenca-Acuna, C. Peery, R. P. Martin, and T. D. Nguyen. Planetp: Using gossiping to build content addressable peer-to-peer information sharing communities. In *Proc. 12th IEEE Int. Symp. High Performance Distributed Computing*, pages 236–249, 2003. DOI: 10.1109/HPDC.2003.1210033 Cited on page(s) 64

F. Dabek, M. F. Kaashoek, D. R. Karger, R. Morris, and I. Stoica. Wide-area cooperative storage with CFS. In *Proc. 18th ACM Symp. on Operating System Principles*, pages 202–215, 2001. DOI: 10.1145/502034.502054 Cited on page(s) 17

G. Das, D. Gunopulos, N. Koudas, and N. Sarkas. Ad-hoc top-k query answering for data streams. In *Proc. 33rd Int. Conf. on Very Large Data Bases*, pages 183–194, 2007. Cited on page(s) 57

N. Daswani, H. Garcia-Molina, and B. Yang. Open problems in data-sharing P2P systems. In *Proc. 9th Int. Conf. on Database Theory*, pages 1–15, 2003. Cited on page(s) 3, 30

W. K. Dedzoe, P. Lamarre, R. Akbarinia, and P. Valduriez. Asap top-k query processing in unstructured p2p systems. In *Proc.10th IEEE Int. Conf. on Peer-to-Peer Computing*, pages 1–10, 2010. DOI: 10.1109/P2P.2010.5569974 Cited on page(s) 67, 69

A. J. Demers, D. H. Greene, C. Hauser, W. Irish, J. Larson, S. Shenker, H. E. Sturgis, D. C. Swinehart, and D. B. Terry. Epidemic algorithms for replicated database maintenance. In *Proc. ACM SIGACT-SIGOPS 6th Symp. on the Principles of Distributed Computing*, pages 1–12, 1987. DOI: 10.1145/41840.41841 Cited on page(s) 14

M. El Dick, E. Pacitti, and B. Kemme. Flower-cdn: a hybrid P2P overlay for efficient query processing in CDN. In *Advances in Database Technology, Proc. 12th Int. Conf. on Extending Database Technology*, pages 427–438, 2009. DOI: 10.1145/1516360.1516410 Cited on page(s) 35

M. El Dick, E. Pacitti, R. Akbarinia, and B. Kemme. Building a P2P content distribution network with high performance, scalability and robustness. *Inf. Syst.*, 36(2):222–247, 2011. DOI: 10.1016/j.is.2010.08.007 Cited on page(s) 37

F. Draidi, E. Pacitti, and B. Kemme. P2prec: A p2p recommendation system for large-scale data sharing. *T. Large-Scale Data- and Knowledge-Centered Systems*, 3:87–116, 2011a. DOI: 10.1007/978-3-642-23074-5_4 Cited on page(s) 52

F. Draidi, E. Pacitti, D. Parigot, and G. Verger. P2prec: a social-based p2p recommendation system. In *Proc. 20th ACM Int. Conf. on Information and Knowledge Management*, pages 2593–2596, 2011b. DOI: 10.1145/2063576.2064028 Cited on page(s) 52

P. T. Eugster, R. Guerraoui, A.-M. Kermarrec, and L. Massoulieacute. Epidemic information dissemination in distributed systems. *Comput.*, 37(5):60–67, 2004. DOI: 10.1109/MC.2004.1297243 Cited on page(s) 14

R. Fagin. Combining fuzzy information from multiple systems. *J. Comp. and System Sci.*, 58(1): 83–99, 1999. DOI: 10.1006/jcss.1998.1600 Cited on page(s) 59

R. Fagin, A. Lotem, and M. Naor. Optimal aggregation algorithms for middleware. In *Proc. 20th ACM SIGACT-SIGMOD-SIGART Symp. on Principles of Database Systems*, pages 102–113, 2001. DOI: 10.1145/375551.375567 Cited on page(s) 58

R. Fagin, A. Lotem, and M. Naor. Optimal aggregation algorithms for middleware. *J. Comp. and System Sci.*, 66(4):614–656, 2003. DOI: 10.1016/S0022-0000(03)00026-6 Cited on page(s) 58, 60

F. Le Fessant, S. B. Handurukande, A.-M. Kermarrec, and L. Massoulié. Clustering in P2P file sharing workloads. In *Proc. 3rd Int. Workshop Peer-to-Peer Systems*, pages 217–226, 2004. DOI: 10.1007/978-3-540-30183-7_21 Cited on page(s) 20

M. J. Freedman, E. Freudenthal, and D. Mazières. Democratizing content publication with Coral. In *Proc. 1st USENIX Symp. on Networked Systems Design & Implementation*, pages 239–252, 2004. Cited on page(s) 31, 32

J. Gao and P. Steenkiste. An adaptive protocol for efficient support of range queries in dht-based systems. In *Proc. 12th IEEE Int. Conf. on Network Protocols*, pages 239–250, 2004. DOI: 10.1109/ICNP.2004.1348114 Cited on page(s) 2

H. Garcia-Molina and A. Crespo. Semantic overlay networks for p2p systems. Technical Report 2003-75, Stanford InfoLab, 2003. Cited on page(s) 47

D. Goldberg, D. A. Nichols, B. M. Oki, and D. B. Terry. Using collaborative filtering to weave an information tapestry. *Commun. ACM*, 35(12):61–70, 1992. DOI: 10.1145/138859.138867 Cited on page(s) 42, 43

Z. Guan, G. Yan, and H. Huang. A novel top-k query scheme in unstructured p2p networks. In *Proc. 9th IEEE Int. Conf. on Computer and Information Technology*, pages 16–21, 2009. DOI: 10.1109/CIT.2009.86 Cited on page(s) 67

K. Gummadi, R. Gummadi, S. Gribble, S. Ratnasamy, S. Shenker, and I. Stoica. The impact of dht routing geometry on resilience and proximity. In *Proc. 2003 Conf. on Applications, Technologies, Architectures, and Protocols for Computer Communication*, pages 381–394, 2003. DOI: 10.1145/863955.863998 Cited on page(s) 8

Şule Gündüz-Ögüdücü. *Web Page Recommendation Models: Theory and Algorithms*. Morgan & Claypool, 2010. DOI: 10.2200/S00305ED1V01Y201010DTM010 Cited on page(s) 45

U. Güntzer, W.-T. Balke, and W. Kießling. Optimizing multi-feature queries for image databases. In Amr El Abbadi, Michael L. Brodie, Sharma Chakravarthy, Umeshwar Dayal, Nabil Kamel, Gunter Schlageter, and Kyu-Young Whang, editors, *Proc. 26th Int. Conf. on Very Large Data Bases*, pages 419–428, 2000. Cited on page(s) 58

P. Han, B. Xie, F. Yang, and R. Shen. A scalable p2p recommender system based on distributed collaborative filtering. *Expert Syst. Appl.*, 27(2):203–210, 2004. DOI: 10.1016/j.eswa.2004.01.003 Cited on page(s) 50

S. B. Handurukande, A.-M. Kermarrec, F. Le Fessant, and L. Massoulié. Exploiting semantic clustering in the eDonkey P2P network. In *Proc. 11th ACM SIGOPS European Workshop*, page 20, 2004. DOI: 10.1145/1133572.1133612 Cited on page(s) 20

M. Harren, J. M. Hellerstein, R. Huebsch, B. Thau Loo, S. Shenker, and I. Stoica. Complex queries in dht-based peer-to-peer networks. In *Proc. 1st Int. Workshop Peer-to-Peer Systems*, pages 242–259, 2002. Cited on page(s) 2

G. R. Hjaltason and H. Samet. Index-driven similarity search in metric spaces. *ACM Trans. Database Syst.*, 28(4):517–580, 2003. DOI: 10.1145/958942.958948 Cited on page(s) 57

R. Huebsch, J. M. Hellerstein, N. Lanham, B. Thau Loo, S. Shenker, and I. Stoica. Querying the internet with pier. In *Proc. 29th Int. Conf. on Very Large Data Bases*, pages 321–332, 2003. Cited on page(s) 2

A. Iamnitchi and I. T. Foster. Interest-aware information dissemination in small-world communities. In *Proc. 14th IEEE Int. Symp. High Performance Distributed Computing*, pages 167–175, 2005. DOI: 10.1109/HPDC.2005.1520954 Cited on page(s) 48

A. Iamnitchi, M. Ripeanu, and I. T. Foster. Locating data in (small-world?) peer-to-peer scientific collaborations. In *Proc. 1st Int. Workshop Peer-to-Peer Systems*, pages 232–241, 2002. Cited on page(s) 47

S. Iyer, A. I. T. Rowstron, and P. Druschel. Squirrel: a decentralized P2P web cache. In *Proc. ACM SIGACT-SIGOPS 21st Symp. on the Principles of Distributed Computing*, pages 213–222, 2002. Cited on page(s) 33

M. Jelasity and Ö. Babaoglu. T-Man: Gossip-based overlay topology management. In *Proc. 3rd Int. Workshop on Engineering Self-Organising Systems*, pages 1–15, 2005. DOI: 10.1016/j.comnet.2009.03.013 Cited on page(s) 16

M. Jelasity, R. Guerraoui, A.-M. Kermarrec, and M. van Steen. The peer sampling service: experimental evaluation of unstructured gossip-based implementations. In *Proc. ACM/IFIP/USENIX 5th Int. Middleware Conf.*, pages 79–98, 2004. Cited on page(s) 16

C. Jin, K. Yi, L. Chen, J. Xu Yu, and X. Lin. Sliding-window top-k queries on uncertain streams. *VLDB J.*, 19(3):411–435, 2010. DOI: 10.1007/s00778-009-0171-0 Cited on page(s) 57

H. Jin, X. Ning, and H. Chen. Efficient search for peer-to-peer information retrieval using semantic small world. In *Proc. 15th Int. World Wide Web Conf.*, pages 1003–1004, 2006. DOI: 10.1145/1135777.1135986 Cited on page(s) 47

V. Kalogeraki, D. Gunopulos, and D. Zeinalipour-Yazti. A local search mechanism for peer-to-peer networks. In *Proc. 11th Int. Conf. on Information and Knowledge Management*, pages 300–307, 2002. DOI: 10.1145/584792.584842 Cited on page(s) 5

A.-M. Kermarrec and M. van Steen. Gossiping in distributed systems. *Operating Systems Rev.*, 41 (5):2–7, 2007. DOI: 10.1145/1317379.1317381 Cited on page(s) 14, 17

AM Kermarrec, V. Leroy, A. Moin, and C. Thraves. Application of random walks to decentralized recommender systems. In *Proc. 14th Int. Conf. Principles of Distributed Systems*, pages 48–63, 2010. DOI: 10.1007/978-3-642-17653-1_4 Cited on page(s) 50

I. A. Klampanos and J. M. Jose. An architecture for information retrieval over semi-collaborating peer-to-peer networks. In *Proc. 2004 ACM Symp. on Applied Computing*, pages 1078–1083, 2004. DOI: 10.1145/967900.968119 Cited on page(s) 47

N. Koudas, B. Chin Ooi, K.-L. Tan, and R. Zhang. Approximate nn queries on streams with guaranteed error/performance bounds. In *Proc. 30th Int. Conf. on Very Large Data Bases*, pages 804–815, 2004. Cited on page(s) 57

B. Krishnamurthy, J. Wang, and Y. Xie. Early measurements of a cluster-based architecture for P2P systems. In *Proc. 1st ACM SIGCOMM Workshop on Internet Measurement*, pages 105–109, 2001. DOI: 10.1145/505202.505216 Cited on page(s) 19

J. Kubiatowicz, D. Bindel, Y. Chen, S. E. Czerwinski, P. R. Eaton, D. Geels, R. Gummadi, S. C. Rhea, H. Weatherspoon, W. Weimer, C. Wells, and B. Y. Zhao. Oceanstore: An architecture for global-scale persistent storage. In *Proc. 9th Int. Conf. on Architectural Support for Programming Languages and Operating Systems*, pages 190–201, 2000. DOI: 10.1145/356989.357007 Cited on page(s) 2

S. Larson, C. Snow, and V. Pande. Folding@home and genome@home: using distributed computing to tackle previously intractable problems in computational biology. In R. Grant, editor, *Modern Methods in Computational Biology*. Horizon Press, 2003a. Cited on page(s) 1

S. M. Larson, C. D. Snow, M. Shirts, and V. S. Pande. Folding@home and genome@home: Using distributed computing to tackle previously intractable problems in computational biology. *Computational Genomics J.*, 2003b. Cited on page(s) 1

F. Li, K. Yi, and W. Le. Top-*k* queries on temporal data. *VLDB J.*, 19(5):715–733, 2010. DOI: 10.1007/s00778-010-0186-6 Cited on page(s) 57

X. Li and J. Wu. Searching techniques in peer-to-peer networks. In W. Zheng, X. Liu, S. Shi, J. Hu, and H. Dong, editors, *Handbook of Theoretical and Algorithmic Aspects of Ad Hoc, Sensor, and Peer-to-Peer Networks*. Auerbach Publications, 2006. Cited on page(s) 4

J. Liang, R. Kumar, and K. W. Ross. The fasttrack overlay: A measurement study. *Computer Networks*, 50(6):842–858, 2006. DOI: 10.1016/j.comnet.2005.07.014 Cited on page(s) 46

G. Linden, B. Smith, and J. York. Industry report: Amazon.com recommendations: Item-to-item collaborative filtering. *IEEE Distributed Systems Online*, 4(1), 2003. DOI: 10.1109/MIC.2003.1167344 Cited on page(s) 44

P. Linga, I. Gupta, and K. Birman. A churn-resistant P2P web caching system. In *Proc. ACM Workshop on Survivable and Self-Regenerative Systems*, pages 1–10, 2003. DOI: 10.1145/1036921.1036922 Cited on page(s) 34, 35

Y. Liu, L. Xiao, X. Liu, L. M. Ni, and X. Zhang. Location awareness in unstructured P2P systems. *IEEE Trans. Parall. Dist. Sys.*, 16(2):163–174, 2005. DOI: 10.1109/TPDS.2005.21 Cited on page(s) 19

J. Lv and X. Cheng. Wongoo: A pure peer-to-peer full text information retrieval system based on semantic overlay networks. In *Proc. 3rd IEEE Int. Symp. on Network Computing and Applications*, pages 47–54, 2004. DOI: 10.1109/NCA.2004.1347761 Cited on page(s) 47

Q. Lv, P. Cao, E. Cohen, K. Li, and S. Shenker. Search and replication in unstructured peer-to-peer networks. In *Proc. 16th Annual Int. Conf. on Supercmputing*, pages 84–95, 2002. DOI: 10.1145/514191.514206 Cited on page(s) 6

D. Malkhi, M. Naor, and D. Ratajczak. Viceroy: a scalable and dynamic emulation of the butterfly. In *Proc. ACM SIGACT-SIGOPS 21st Symp. on the Principles of Distributed Computing*, pages 183–192, 2002. DOI: 10.1145/571825.571857 Cited on page(s) 11

T. W. Malone, J. Yates, and R. I. Benjamin. Electronic markets and electronic hierarchies. *Commun. ACM*, 30(6):484–497, 1987. DOI: 10.1145/214762.214766 Cited on page(s) 42

B. Maniymaran, M. Bertier, and A.-M. Kermarrec. Build one, get one free: Leveraging the coexistence of multiple P2P overlay networks. In *Proc. 27th Int. Conf. on Distributed Computing Systems*, page 33, 2007. DOI: 10.1109/ICDCS.2007.88 Cited on page(s) 21

S. Marti, P. G., and H. Garcia-Molina. Sprout: P2p routing with social networks. In *Advances in Database Technology, Proc. 9th Int. Conf. on Extending Database Technology*, pages 425–435, 2004. Cited on page(s) 48

P. Massa and P. Avesani. Trust-aware collaborative filtering for recommender systems. In *Proc. Int. Conf. on Cooperative Inf. Syst.*, pages 492–508, 2004. DOI: 10.1007/978-3-540-30468-5_31 Cited on page(s) 44, 51

M. R. McLaughlin and J. L. Herlocker. A collaborative filtering algorithm and evaluation metric that accurately model the user experience. In *Proc. 27th Annual Int. ACM SIGIR Conf. on Research and Development in Information Retrieval*, pages 329–336, 2004. DOI: 10.1145/1008992.1009050 Cited on page(s) 42

D. A. Menascé and L. Kanchanapalli. Probabilistic scalable p2p resource location services. *Perf. Eval. Rev.*, 30(2):48–58, 2002. DOI: 10.1145/588160.588167 Cited on page(s) 8

S. Michel, P. Triantafillou, and G. Weikum. Klee: A framework for distributed top-k query algorithms. In *Proc. 31st Int. Conf. on Very Large Data Bases*, pages 637–648, 2005. Cited on page(s) 64

B. N. Miller, J. A. Konstan, and J. Riedl. Pocketlens: Toward a personal recommender system. *ACM Trans. Information Syst.*, 22(3):437–476, 2004. DOI: 10.1145/1010614.1010618 Cited on page(s) 49

C. Mohan. Caching technologies for Web applications. In *Proc. 27th Int. Conf. on Very Large Data Bases*, page 726, 2001. Cited on page(s) 25, 26

W. Nejdl, W. Siberski, and M. Sintek. Design issues and challenges for rdf- and schema-based peer-to-peer systems. *ACM SIGMOD Rec.*, 32(3):41–46, 2003. DOI: 10.1145/945721.945731 Cited on page(s) 3

S. Nepal and M. V. Ramakrishna. Query processing issues in image (multimedia) databases. In *Proc. 15th Int. Conf. on Data Engineering*, pages 22–29, 1999. DOI: 10.1109/ICDE.1999.754894 Cited on page(s) 58

W. Siong Ng, B. Chin Ooi, K.-L. Tan, and A. Zhou. Peerdb: A p2p-based system for distributed data sharing. In *Proc. 19th Int. Conf. on Data Engineering*, pages 633–644, 2003. DOI: 10.1109/ICDE.2003.1260827 Cited on page(s) 1

N. Ntarmos and P. Triantafillou. Aesop: altruism-endowed self-organizing peers. In *Proc. 2nd Workshop on Databases, Information Systems, and Peer-to-Peer Computing*, pages 151–165, 2004. DOI: 10.1007/978-3-540-31838-5_11 Cited on page(s) 22

Venkata N. Padmanabhan and Kunwadee Sripanidkulchai. The case for cooperative networking. In *Proc. 1st Int. Workshop Peer-to-Peer Systems*, pages 178–190, 2002. Cited on page(s) 32

V. S. Pai, L. Wang, K. Park, R. Pang, and L. Peterson. The dark side of the Web: an open proxy's view. *Comp. Comm. Rev.*, 34(1):57–62, 2004. DOI: 10.1145/972374.972385 Cited on page(s) 31

G. Pallis and A. Vakali. Insight and perspectives for content delivery networks. *Commun. ACM*, 49 (1):101–106, 2006. DOI: 10.1145/1107458.1107462 Cited on page(s) 25, 27

M. J. Pazzani and D. Billsus. Learning and revising user profiles: The identification of interesting web sites. *Machine Learning*, 27(3):313–331, 1997. DOI: 10.1023/A:1007369909943 Cited on page(s) 45

W. Rao, L. Chen, A. W. Fu, and Y. Bu. Optimal proactive caching in P2P network: analysis and application. In *Proc. 16th ACM Int. Conf. on Information and Knowledge Management*, pages 663–672, 2007. DOI: 10.1145/1321440.1321533 Cited on page(s) 33

S. Ratnasamy, P. Francis, M. Handley, R. M. Karp, and S. Shenker. A scalable content-addressable network. In *Proc. Conf. on Applications, Technologies, Architectures, and Protocols for Computer Communication*, pages 161–172, 2001. DOI: 10.1145/383059.383072 Cited on page(s) 2, 10, 17, 47

S. Ratnasamy, M. Handley, R. M. Karp, and S. Shenker. Topologically-aware overlay construction and server selection. In *Proc. 21st Annual Joint Conf. of the IEEE Computer and Communication Societies*, pages 1190–1199, 2002a. DOI: 10.1109/INFCOM.2002.1019369 Cited on page(s) 19

S. Ratnasamy, I. Stoica, and S. Shenker. Routing algorithms for DHTs: Some open questions. In *Proc. 1st Int. Workshop Peer-to-Peer Systems*, pages 45–52, 2002b. Cited on page(s) 19

R. Van Renesse, Y. Minsky, and M. Hayden. A gossip-style failure detection service. Technical report TR98-1687, Cornell University, 1998. Cited on page(s) 15

P. Resnick and H. R. Varian. Recommender systems - introduction to the special section. *Commun. ACM*, 40(3):56–58, 1997. DOI: 10.1145/245108.245121 Cited on page(s) 42

P. Resnick, N. Iacovou, M. Suchak, P. Bergstrom, and J. Riedl. Grouplens: An open architecture for collaborative filtering of netnews. In *Proc 1994 Conf. on Computer Supported Cooperative Work*, pages 175–186, 1994. DOI: 10.1145/192844.192905 Cited on page(s) 43, 44

Sean C. Rhea and John Kubiatowicz. Probabilistic location and routing. In *Proc. 21st Annual Joint Conf. of the IEEE Computer and Communication Societies*, pages 1248– 1257, 2002. DOI: 10.1109/INFCOM.2002.1019375 Cited on page(s) 8

M. Ripeanu, I. T. Foster, and A. Iamnitchi. Mapping the Gnutella network: Properties of large-scale P2P systems and implications for system design. *IEEE Internet Comput.*, 6(1):50–57, 2002a. Cited on page(s) 18

M. Ripeanu, A. Iamnitchi, and I. T. Foster. Mapping the gnutella network. *IEEE Internet Comput.*, 6(1):50–57, 2002b. DOI: 10.1109/4236.978369 Cited on page(s) 64

A. Rowstron and P. Druschel. Pastry: Scalable, decentralized object location, and routing for large-scale P2P systems. In *Proc. ACM/IFIP/USENIX 5th Int. Middleware Conf.*, pages 329–350, 2001a. Cited on page(s) 19

A. I. T. Rowstron and P. Druschel. Pastry: Scalable, decentralized object location, and routing for large-scale peer-to-peer systems. In *Proc. IFIP/ACM Int. Conf. on Distributed Systems Platforms*, pages 329–350, 2001b. Cited on page(s) 2, 12

A. I. T. Rowstron and P. Druschel. Storage management and caching in past, a large-scale, persistent peer-to-peer storage utility. In *Proc. 18th ACM Symp. on Operating System Principles*, pages 188–201, 2001c. DOI: 10.1145/502034.502053 Cited on page(s) 2

A. I. T. Rowstron and P. Druschel. Storage management and caching in PAST, a large-scale, persistent peer-to-peer storage utility. *Proc. 18th ACM Symp. on Operating System Principles*, pages 188–201, 2001d. DOI: 10.1145/502034.502053 Cited on page(s) 17

Y.-S. Ryu and S.-B. Yang. An effective P2P web caching system under dynamic participation of peers. *IEICE Trans.*, 88-B(4):1476–1483, 2005. Cited on page(s) 32

O. D. Sahin, F. Emekçi, D. Agrawal, and A. El Abbadi. Content-based similarity search over peer-to-peer systems. In *Proc. 2nd Workshop on Databases, Information Systems, and Peer-to-Peer Computing*, pages 61–78, 2004. Cited on page(s) 47

S. Saroiu, P. Krishna Gummadi, R. J. Dunn, S. D. Gribble, and H. M. Levy. An analysis of Internet content delivery systems. In *Proc. 5th USENIX Symp. on Operating System Design and Implementation*, pages 315–327, 2002. DOI: 10.1145/1060289.1060319 Cited on page(s) 18, 25

B. M. Sarwar, G. Karypis, J. A. Konstan, and J. Riedl. Item-based collaborative filtering recommendation algorithms. In *Proc. 10th Int. World Wide Web Conf.*, pages 285–295, 2001. DOI: 10.1145/371920.372071 Cited on page(s) 44

A. I. Schein, A. Popescul, L. H. Ungar, and D. M. Pennock. Methods and metrics for cold-start recommendations. In *Proc. 25th Annual Int. ACM SIGIR Conf. on Research and Development in Information Retrieval*, pages 253–260, 2002. DOI: 10.1145/564376.564421 Cited on page(s) 44

M. Schlosser, M. Sintek, S. Decker, and W. Nejdl. Hypercup. Technical report, Stanford University, 2002. Cited on page(s) 12

U. Shardanand and P. Maes. Social information filtering: Algorithms for automating "word of mouth." In *Proc. SIGCHI Conf. on Human Factors in Computing Systems*, pages 210–217, 1995. DOI: 10.1145/223904.223931 Cited on page(s) 43

Haiying Shen and Cheng-Zhong Xu. Hash-based proximity clustering for efficient load balancing in heterogeneous DHT networks. *J. Parall. and Distrib. Comput.*, 68(5):686–702, 2008. DOI: 10.1016/j.jpdc.2007.10.005 Cited on page(s) 22

A. Shepitsen, J. Gemmell, B. Mobasher, and R. D. Burke. Personalized recommendation in social tagging systems using hierarchical clustering. In *Proc. 2nd ACM Conf. on Recommender Systems*, pages 259–266, 2008. DOI: 10.1145/1454008.1454048 Cited on page(s) 46

M. A. Soliman, I. F. Ilyas, and K. Chen-Chuan Chang. Top-k query processing in uncertain databases. In *Proc. 23rd Int. Conf. on Data Engineering*, pages 896–905, 2007. DOI: 10.1109/ICDE.2007.367935 Cited on page(s) 57

Y. J. Song, V. Ramasubramanian, and E. G. Sirer. Optimal resource utilization in content distribution networks. Technical report TR2005-2004, Cornell University, 2005. Cited on page(s) 31

K. Sripanidkulchai, B. M. Maggs, and H. Zhang. Efficient content location using interest-based locality in peer-to-peer systems. In *Proc. 22nd Annual Joint Conf. of the IEEE Computer and Communication Societies*, 2003a. DOI: 10.1109/INFCOM.2003.1209237 Cited on page(s) 48

K. Sripanidkulchai, B. M. Maggs, and Hui Zhang. Efficient content location using interest-based locality in P2P systems. In *Proc. 22nd Annual Joint Conf. of the IEEE Computer and Communication Societies*, pages 2166–2176, 2003b. DOI: 10.1109/INFCOM.2003.1209237 Cited on page(s) 20, 48

T. Stading, P. Maniatis, and M. Baker. P2P caching schemes to address flash crowds. In *Proc. 1st Int. Workshop Peer-to-Peer Systems*, pages 203–213, 2002. Cited on page(s) 33

A. Stavrou, D. Rubenstein, and S. Sahu. A lightweight, robust P2P system to handle flash crowds. In *Proc. 10th IEEE Int. Conf. on Network Protocols*, page 226, 2002. DOI: 10.1109/ICNP.2002.1181410 Cited on page(s) 33

I. Stoica, R. Morris, D. R. Karger, M. F. Kaashoek, and H. Balakrishnan. Chord: A scalable peer-to-peer lookup service for internet applications. In *Proc. 2001 Conf. on Applications, Technologies, Architectures, and Protocols for Computer Communication*, pages 149–160, 2001. DOI: 10.1145/964723.383071 Cited on page(s) 2, 10

C. Tang, Z. Xu, and M. Mahalingam. psearch: information retrieval in structured overlays. *Computer Communication Review*, 33(1):89–94, 2003. DOI: 10.1145/774763.774777 Cited on page(s) 47

Akamai Technologies. Akamai - the business Internet - a predictable platform for profitable e-business. White paper, 2004. http://www.akamai.com/dl/Whitepapers/Akamai_Business_Internet_Whitepaper.pdf. Cited on page(s) 28

T. Tran, H. Wang, S. Rudolph, and P. Cimiano. Top-k exploration of query candidates for efficient keyword search on graph-shaped (rdf) data. In *Proc. 25th Int. Conf. on Data Engineering*, pages 405–416, 2009. DOI: 10.1109/ICDE.2009.119 Cited on page(s) 57

K. H. L. Tso-Sutter, L. Balby Marinho, and L. Schmidt-Thieme. Tag-aware recommender systems by fusion of collaborative filtering algorithms. In *Proc. 2008 ACM Symp. on Applied Computing*, pages 1995–1999, 2008. DOI: 10.1145/1363686.1364171 Cited on page(s) 46

D. Tsoumakos and N. Roussopoulos. Adaptive probabilistic search (aps) for peer-to-peer networks. Technical report, University of Maryland, 2003a. Cited on page(s) 6

D. Tsoumakos and N. Roussopoulos. A comparison of peer-to-peer search methods. In *Proc. 6th Int. Workshop on the World Wide Web and Databases*, pages 61–66, 2003b. Cited on page(s) 5

Y. Upadrashta, J. Vassileva, and W. K. Grassmann. Social networks in peer-to-peer systems. In *Proc. 38th Annual Hawaii Int. Conf. on System Sciences*, 2005. DOI: 10.1109/HICSS.2005.546 Cited on page(s) 48

A. Vlachou, C. Doulkeridis, K. Nørvåg, and M. Vazirgiannis. On efficient top-k query processing in highly distributed environments. In *Proc. ACM SIGMOD Int. Conf. on Management of Data*, pages 753–764, 2008. DOI: 10.1145/1376616.1376692 Cited on page(s) 69

S. Voulgaris and M. van Steen. Epidemic-style management of semantic overlays for content-based searching. In *Proc. 11th Int. Euro-Par Conf.*, pages 1143–1152, 2005. DOI: 10.1007/11549468 Cited on page(s) 16

S. Voulgaris, D. Gavidia, and M. Steen. Cyclon: Inexpensive membership management for unstructured p2p overlays. *J. Network Syst. Manage.*, 13(2):197–217, 2005. DOI: 10.1007/s10922-005-4441-x Cited on page(s) 16

M. Waldman, A. D. Rubin, and L. Faith Cranor. Publius: A robust, tamper-evident, censorship-resistant, web publishing system. In *USENIX Security Symposium*, pages 59–72, 2000. Cited on page(s) 3

J. Wang. A survey of Web caching schemes for the Internet. *Comp. Comm. Rev.*, 29(5):36–46, 1999. DOI: 10.1145/505696.505701 Cited on page(s) 25, 26

X. Wang, W. S. Ng, B. C. Ooi, K. Tan, and A. Zhou. Buddyweb: A P2P-based collaborative web caching system. In *Web Engineering and Peer-to-Peer Computing, Networking 2002 Workshops*, pages 247–251, 2002. DOI: 10.1007/3-540-45745-3_22 Cited on page(s) 33

G. Wiederhold. Mediators in the architecture of future information systems. *Comput.*, 25(3):38–49, 1992. DOI: 10.1109/2.121508 Cited on page(s) 13

M. Wu, J. Xu, X. Tang, and W.-C. Lee. Monitoring top-k query in wireless sensor networks. In *Proc. 22nd Int. Conf. on Data Engineering*, page 143, 2006. DOI: 10.1109/TKDE.2007.1038 Cited on page(s) 57

B. Yang and H. Garcia-Molina. Improving search in peer-to-peer networks. In *Proc. 22nd Int. Conf. on Distributed Computing Systems*, pages 5–14, 2002. DOI: 10.1109/ICDCS.2002.1022237 Cited on page(s) 5, 7

D. Zeinalipour-Yazti, Z. Vagena, D. Gunopulos, V. Kalogeraki, V. J. Tsotras, M. Vlachos, N. Koudas, and D. Srivastava. The threshold join algorithm for top-k queries in distributed sensor networks. In *Proc. 2nd Workshop on Data Management for Sensor Networks*, pages 61–66, 2005. DOI: 10.1145/1080885.1080896 Cited on page(s) 62

B. Y. Zhao, L. Huang, J. Stribling, S. C. Rhea, A. D. Joseph, and J. Kubiatowicz. Tapestry: a resilient global-scale overlay for service deployment. *IEEE J. Selected Areas in Comm.*, 22(1):41–53, 2004. DOI: 10.1109/JSAC.2003.818784 Cited on page(s) 2, 9, 19

CN. Ziegler, S. M. McNee, J. A. Konstan, and G. Lausen. Improving recommendation lists through topic diversification. In *Proc. 14th Int. World Wide Web Conf.*, pages 22–32, 2005. DOI: 10.1145/1060745.1060754 Cited on page(s) 42

Authors' Biographies

ESTHER PACITTI

Esther Pacitti is a professor of computer science at University of Montpellier 2 pursuing research in large-scale distributed data management and head of a research team at Lirmm (University of Montpellier 2). She has served or is serving as program committee member of major international conferences and has edited an co-authored several books. She has also published a significant amount of technical papers and journal papers in well-known international conferences and journals.

REZA AKBARINIA

Reza Akbarinia is a research scientist at INRIA, France. He received his Ph.D. degree in Computer Science from the University of Nantes in 2007. His research focuses on data management in large-scale distributed systems (P2P, grid, cloud), in particular, query processing, uncertain data management, replication, etc. He has authored and co-authored several technical papers in main database conferences and journals, and has served as PC member in several important international conferences.

MANAL EL-DICK

Manal El-Dick received M.S. and Ph.D. degrees in computer science from the University of Nantes, France in 2006 and 2010, respectively. She is currently Associate Professor at the Lebanese University. Her research interests focus on practical and scalable protocols to cope with the recent and tremendous evolution of distributed systems. She is the author and co-author of several publications in peer-reviewed journals and international conferences.